BUILDING BULLETIN 71

The Outdoor Classroom

EDUCATIONAL USE, LANDSCAPE DESIGN & MANAGEMENT OF SCHOOL GROUNDS

LONDON: HMSO

ACKNOWLEDGEMENTS

The co-authors of this *Building Bulletin*, Brian Billimore, John Brooke, Rupert Booth and Keith Funnell, wish to thank all those who have advised on the contents and contributed during its preparation, and the schools that have provided exemplar information and photographs.

The material contained in the publication draws on the research of the Learning through Landscapes project sponsored by the Department of Education and Science, the Countryside Commission and a consortium of eleven Local Authorities. Initially set up in 1986, the project is now a charitable trust and will continue to explore the use of school grounds as an educational resource.

Foreword

1. This Bulletin describes the range of possible educational uses of school grounds and how the necessary resources may be created and managed. It is aimed at all those involved in the educational use and the consequent design and management of grounds – pupils, teachers, governors, parents, voluntary and community groups, inspectors and advisers, architects, landscape architects, landscape managers and playing field officers. It seeks to heighten their awareness of the potential contribution that appropriately designed and managed grounds can make to teaching and learning and highlights the value of a multidisciplinary approach.

2. The evolving curriculum poses challenges to everyone concerned with teaching. The implementation of the National Curriculum, the greater emphasis on practical activities and the need for teachers to make the presentation of learning material relevant for pupils all have implications for the full use of available space within the school boundaries. Grounds and buildings should complement each other to provide a well-designed and stimulating environment that influences and inspires the generations of pupils who receive their education there.

3. The Learning through Landscapes project found a growing realisation of the potential of the grounds as a highly valuable resource that can support and enrich a school's curriculum and the education of its pupils. The following sections demonstrate how both educational opportunity and environmental quality can be improved.

Executive Summary

Purpose and Background

The aim of this publication is to highlight the potential of school grounds as a valuable resource that can support and enrich the whole curriculum and the education of all pupils. It draws directly on the recent research done by the Learning through Landscapes project, which established that much learning, common to a variety of curriculum areas, can be promoted strongly and naturally outside. In order to maximise such opportunities the scale and character of spaces should relate far more closely to the needs of pupils and more variety should be created in the outdoor environment.

Educational Use

School grounds can provide a wealth of interest and resources for both personal and social education. The National Curriculum can be supported to some degree by studies outdoors, and a number of these are cross-curricular. Such direct experience in observation, investigation and participation in design and development of grounds helps pupils to be informed, responsible and enterprising. The nature of the grounds also has a profound effect upon activities outside lesson time, and on the attitudes of pupils towards their environment. The reinforcement of knowledge resulting from exploration and the use of imagination and from sharing and caring is that much greater where the design and management of the grounds is completely responsive to the widest possible spectrum of educational use.

Qualities and Features

The landscape around the school is a potentially malleable resource that can be remodelled over time to meet the changing demands placed upon it. The grounds should express an individual identity based on the character of the local environment. Where there is a mature landscape, changes can still be made, even to the extent of undoing or remaking changes brought about through earlier initiatives. It is important not to determine what will happen in each and every part of the grounds, but to create a varied and flexible landscape that will afford countless opportunities, some expected and others which have not been envisaged. In most school grounds there is a need for contrasting spaces of varying sizes and qualities which can appeal to different individuals and accommodate different uses.

Roles and Relationships

Achievement of these objectives is dependent on a partnership of educational and landscaping skills and a teamwork approach. A divergence of objectives and the lack of a common purpose has been a major impediment to progress. There are many examples of individual initiatives, but they are richer and more lasting where they involve teachers and pupils educational advisers and landscape specialists. Communication and commitment is the key and everyone concerned should be invited to participate. A close working relationship between landscape designers and managers is vital, since designers influence the nature and type of management and managers influence the establishment of a new landscape scheme.

New School Sites

In the brief for a new school site, the landscape deserves as much attention as the building. Beyond the need to state size of areas and number of facilities, it should explain the aims and aspirations of teachers and pupils and the character, qualities and features to be created for maximum educational opportunity. Careful appraisal of the site and layout options is necessary, since the most fundamental issue is the overall pattern of development and not the detailed treatment. Outdoor educational provision should be viewed in the context of the external works budget as a whole and not simply planting. There must be a balanced financial allocation to ensure the landscape scheme is adequately resourced with sufficient allowance for aftercare.

Existing School Grounds

The process of enriching existing school grounds should involve pupils and teachers at the earliest stages. Indeed the school should develop its own ideas about outdoor resources and their uses. These should encompass the whole of the grounds (and possibly beyond) and allow for use throughout the year and across the curriculum. Site meetings with educational advisers and landscape staff can then lead to the preparation of a development plan which might establish a range of possibilities and a programme for implementation. This process should allow for long-term changes in the grounds in successive years so that pupils might gain from the anticipation, planning and implementation of new initiatives.

Management and Maintenance

Without specific guidelines and regular user involvement, grounds maintenance has tended to follow a convenient and essentially static regime. Educational use should determine the type and pattern of maintenance and the school should be the prime mover, with the advice and support of landscape staff. Enrichment of outdoor resources does not necessarily mean an increase in the revenue budget and quite often small savings may accrue. A programme of gradual improvement which allows for participation of pupils and teachers is more realistic in terms of funding and is more likely to stimulate change. Some comparative informtion on capital and revenue costs on hard and soft landscapes is included.

Contents

Figures

Introduction

1. In England there are some 24,000 schools and 60,000 – 70,000 hectares of grounds. It has been estimated that the cost of grounds maintenance alone is of the order of £110 million a year. Land is provided by statute to permit not only the provision of buildings but also recreation areas and playing fields. The details are set down in the Education (School Premises) Regulations 1981 (SI 1981 No. 909) and these Regulations have been clarified in *Building Bulletin 28*, 'Playing Fields and Hard Surface Areas', published in 1982. Although outdoor education gets a specific mention in the Regulations, the land has in many instances only been developed for physical education. This must continue to be of vital importance, but the aim is to seek greater diversity of use within the framework provided by *Building Bulletin 28*.

2. Most schools strive to make their indoor teaching and non-teaching areas stimulating and inspiring places. A theme is sometimes allowed to take over the classroom and its environs completely. The most successful themes may run for several weeks and various stimuli, such as two- and three-dimensional wall displays, interesting artifacts and models, may accumulate as the investigations, explorations and discoveries follow their course. Outside the school building the situation is frequently quite different. All too often the grounds are bleak and exposed. Apart from the extensive use made of playing fields and hard-play areas for physical education, the grounds are often under-utilised as an educational resource.

3. Ventures outside the classroom may usefully stimulate cross-curricular work in a variety of subject areas and support and complement work done inside the classroom or provide opportunities for learning which cannot take place inside. Motivation may be strengthened since outdoor learning is likely to be more practically based. There is much learning, common to a variety of curricular areas, that can be promoted strongly and naturally outside. This includes communication skills, problem solving, observation, identification and classification. It has been noted that such skills improve as pupils see more purpose and relevance in first-hand experiences

The outdoor classroom – a sheep shearing demonstration can be organised in the grounds.

Classwork – the wool can then be spun in the classroom

outside. By enhancing the opportunities for learning in the grounds, the range of work is enriched and the potential for direct practical application much increased.

4. The Learning through Landscapes project's research has identified many schools where the grounds have been developed and used as a resource for teaching and learning to support a wider range of curricular studies. It has confirmed that the grounds in which the school stands are a valuable asset. However, grounds maintenance practices have not always been completely in tune with the educational requirements of the curriculum. The need for better collaboration between schools, their advisers and other agencies has been recognised.

5. The research also indicated that the scale and range of spaces inside and outside should relate more closely to the needs of the developing child, and that more variety should be provided in the outdoor environment. This might include sheltered bays where small groups of children can gather to occupy themselves quietly in a pursuit which may be self-chosen or may be part of a curriculum-based activity. Larger sheltered spaces can enable groups of class size to work together. Extensive open spaces can provide for field games and other events, which may be anything from a celebration of a seasonal festival to a hot air balloon launching.

6. There are schools where provision for child-chosen activities, including unsupervised play, is made, although these are comparatively rare. More commonly, unsupervised play is not well provided for and 'playtime' is seen to take place in dull playgrounds, often supervised by other than the qualified teaching staff. The outstanding exceptions where thoughtful provision is made include play environments with equipment, stimulating artifacts and arrangements for quiet gathering places where individuals and small groups can meet.

7. In many schools where the grounds have been developed and used as an educational resource this has usually been achieved by enthusiastic teachers, often in co-operation with pupils, parents and the local education authority, and sometimes with the help of members of the community and other outside agencies. It may have started with ideas about extending the learning from the classroom to outdoors, as a consequence of which the need for changes in the landscape has been identified and work on the school grounds has begun. Such curriculum-led change has taken teachers and pupils outside and the development of the grounds has been closely related to learning needs. In other cases change has been resource-led, where anything from a small part of the grounds to the whole site has been enriched with new features and improved qualities by seeding, planting and other landscape works. Generally it has proved more successful to provide for recognised curricular needs than to create resources and then contemplate their uses.

8. The ensuing description of the educational use of school grounds contains more examples from the primary phase than from secondary. Primary schools have tended to use their grounds more extensively and in a greater variety of ways than secondary schools where the use of the grounds is at a more embryonic stage. The reasons for these differences may relate to the relative sizes of both the schools and their grounds, their approach to the curriculum, and the availability of specialist subject spaces.

9. It hoped that both primary and secondary schools will be able to draw on the information in this Bulletin to make their grounds both more attractive and more educationally useful. Those schools with little or no green spaces can also benefit, albeit at a different scale or in an amended form. Currently about 15% of primary schools have grounds which are almost entirely hard surfaced; this is rare in secondary schools outside London.

Educational Use of School Grounds

1.1 Pupils' impression

The first public building which most children use and come to know intimately is their primary school. Their judgement of design and materials will begin to be formed here, as will their attitudes to stewardship of land and landscape. A large part of the pupil's early education derives from the influence of the building, the grounds and the whole ethos of the school and its organisation. In secondary schools too, grounds can be a valuable resource for subject teaching and a context for the full development of the pupil as a person.

1.2 Learning through Landscapes research

This section is a summary of the ideas and perceptions of the Learning Through Landscapes research team, and their thoughts on the way in which curriculum subjects and cross-curricular work may be supported by studies in suitably developed school grounds. The National Curriculum, with its attainment targets and programmes of study, provides very specific points of reference for purposeful development of grounds to meet curriculum need.

1.3 Physical Education

The subject most commonly associated with the use of school grounds is Physical Education, which has traditionally given strong emphasis to team games and athletics, using them to develop and extend the learning of physical skills, to encourage balanced physical development and to provide opportunities for the improvement of personal and social skills. In more recent times 'fitness stations', 'trim' or 'jogging trails' have been established in some school grounds with the aim

Team games have traditionally been the major reason for providing school grounds.

More recently emphasis has been on challenge to the individual as well as the team and the range of activities has broadened.

of promoting good attitudes to health and physical fitness. However, sports pitches are often exposed and barren in character; this might be relieved by the planting of shelter-belts to create an improved environment for players.

1.4 Outdoor education

Other subjects can also utilise the school grounds. For example, in outdoor education, normally an integral part of the physical education provided in schools, the skills needed for expedition work such as camping, map and compass work and self catering, can be practised in the grounds. Weekend or overnight camps have been run by some schools on their site using the school facilities for cooking, dining and toilet purposes.

1.5 English

In English, the school grounds can provide very rich language experiences which may be sensory and largely concerned with observation and may involve asking questions and undertaking investigations. There is scope within such experiences to use language purposefully and to arrange for the development of specific skills, such as group discussion and negotiation, oral and written reporting, and personal writing in poetry and prose.

Learning and play are indivisible in the use of this hundred square.

Mathematical games on the grass – mobility of resource affords greater opportunities.

The variable growth rate of plants, their diversity of shape and form create many dimensions for study.

Walls offer considerable potential for measuring and estimating, as well as being space dividers or seats.

Different shapes and patterns of hard surface facilitate a range of mathematical project work.

1.6 | Mathematics

In Mathematics there is scope for both work content and practical activity, some of which will help pupils to understand concepts. To take one example, percentages (or fractions) can be understood through measuring the proportions of the grounds showing different characteristics, or by looking at the numbers of different types of trees. At a more advanced level, surveys of materials, living things or human behaviour in the grounds and the consequent analysing of the data can help pupils to understand fundamental statistical concepts. There are also endless opportunities for measuring, estimating, and approximating. In some schools these investigations have become the basis of design work leading to development of the grounds.

Outdoor experiments, with air trapped under a parachute, aid scientific understanding by direct experience.

1.7 Science

There is no difficulty in finding scope within the broad content of National Curriculum science for the use of the school grounds and in finding or developing features which are related to the content of the programmes of study. The grounds have potential for the study of biological, material, earth and physical sciences.

Some schools, for example, have a weather station, a compass rose marked on the school playground or a sun-dial on a plinth or fixed to a south facing wall, which can contribute to a continuous or an occasional study of weather, seasons and time. Basic astronomy (part of the National Curriculum) can be studied if schools can use the night sky viewed from a roof or the grounds without the interference of bright illumination.

Many schools are finding that their own grounds can provide possibilities for continuous ecological and scientific studies of plants and animals. This can supplement work at a field studies centre or at a unique site. A number of schools have made successful attempts to increase the variety of animal and plant life in their grounds. Small beginnings have gradually grown to encompass a diverse range of resources such as ponds, meadows, woodlands, hedgerows, paddocks, and smallholdings.

Sound levels within and round the school grounds can be measured and assessed.

A sun dial provides a historical time machine and aids an understanding of the earth's rotation.

Kite flying highlights the direction, power and variability of the wind.

Other science studies seen in the project included flight, using hot air balloons, rockets, parachutes, movement and travel propulsion (sometimes in connection with physical education). Projects on sound may include testing sound velocity using a large outdoor wall.

1.8 Technology and Design

Technology and design activities will also often benefit from the nature and size of the space available outside. One example is that of constructing large models, especially those intended for travel, which can be tested more fully and thoroughly. Several secondary schools have built hovercraft and land yachts and have looked no further than the school grounds to find a test area. The Learning Through Landscapes research identified several projects which could not have been completed as successfully indoors or, like the building of an Iron Age Roundhouse at a middle school in the South West, could only have been done outside. A number of these projects, such as bridge building, have been cross-curricular, embracing the study of

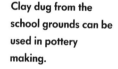

The art of weaving can be developed from raw materials – osiers, reeds and grasses – grown in the grounds.

Clay dug from the school grounds can be used in pottery making.

The construction of a primitive kiln has more meaning when the raw materials are obtained from the grounds.

The construction of Iron Age buildings and enclosures in the grounds brings history to life.

structures, of suitable materials and of mechanics, such as the properties of levers, balances, fulcra and cantilevers. A forestry project has included coppice crafts, tree felling and converting timber for use in furniture making. The principles of primitive building construction can be introduced, together with smaller scale experiments in power generation from wind and water or making control mechanisms for aiding plant growth.

1.9 Information Technology

In the National Curriculum all subject working groups are encouraged to adopt Information Technology in such a way that pupils become aware of its power and are able to use it. There is much data about the school grounds which can be collected on computers, stored and correlated. This data can then be manipulated and used to assist in developing thoughts and ideas.

1.10 Geography

Geography aims to help pupils make sense of their surroundings and to gain a better appreciation of the variety of physical and human conditions on the Earth's surface and of patterns and processes. These aims can be achieved by studies in the locality of the school, beginning in the school grounds. The grounds provide opportunities to practise the skills of geography and to study environments in miniature. Activities can include the consideration of scale, variation in places and orientation, following and making maps and plans, the study of peoples, movement and their use of space. Concepts such as spatial organisation and the change and shaping of the environment can be included.

Relating features in the school grounds to a map of the site can improve geographical skills.

Samples of different geological rocks can be set into a permanent display or incorporated in a wall.

Construction of an Iron Age ditch fortification also affords an insight into underlying geology and a building material for hut walls.

6

1.11 Environmental education

Environmental education is cross-curricular and can embrace the study through observation and investigations of the school's built and natural environment. There are a number of important aspects of the curriculum, recognised in the work of National Curriculum subject-based groups, which fall between subjects or are elements of a range of subjects.

The list established by the National Curriculum Council includes environmental education, together with education for economic understanding, health education, careers education and citizenship, with personal and social education as an umbrella for all of these. The Council is producing curriculum guidance on all these aspects.

Curiosity about the local environment encourages questioning and problem solving.

Cereals can be grown, harvested and ground into flour by the pupils.

Bee-keeping provides a means of studying social insects, pollination and honey production.

Study of insects demands concentration and good skills of observation; it leads to further investigation in the classroom.

Construction of articificial habitats presents a challenge in design technology and aids an understanding of wildlife.

Maypole dancing has links with beliefs, history and the performing arts.

1.12 History

The study of history can sometimes be enriched by looking at the school buildings and grounds; questioning what was happening there during the period being studied and considering the school in the context of its locality and social history. There might be scope for simple archaeology, field walking and the sifting of soil for evidence. Local archivists and historians can often provide documentation on school sites. Landscapes reveal the story of the place and its people; grounds can be used for dramatic reconstruction of historical events, battles may be simulated, famous meetings enacted; trenches, foxholes, walls and defences can be made; roundhouses can be built; ancient kilns can be constructed and used in the way our forebears used them.

1.13 Religious education

There are many decisions to make in relation to the school environment which raise religious and moral issues for the school community. These are concerned with caring and respect for all living things and for property.

In one school, a range of activities involves the pupils in experiences concerned with birth, life and death. Seeds are sown, cherished and finally the vegetable or fruit harvested. Animals are born and bred, cared for and, if death occurs, the animal's body is treated with respect and reverently buried. No opportunity is lost to develop the children's sense of wonder at the

Animal visits allow first-hand experience of giving and caring.

Milking a goat reverses the process of giving, and encourages respect for animals.

This dead fox and the skeleton of a badger, buried and later unearthed by pupils, hold a variety of educational messages.

The gathering of crops gives meaning to the Harvest Festival and Thanksgiving.

beauty of nature, at the intricate detail and meticulous design in plants and flowers. They are encouraged to observe and to wonder at the arrangements of the colours in a cockerel's plumage, the sheen on the fur of a fox, the intricate yet regular double helical pattern of the seeds in the head of the sunflower. Pupils can be made aware of religion through the observation of ceremony, the celebration of harvest festivals and the keeping of special days. They might celebrate Mothers' Day with daffodils which they were responsible for planting and nurturing.

1.14 Drama

There are several schools where the designers have taken advantage of the land levels and slopes to provide outdoor amphitheatres. Some schools have worked to create distinct spaces through having planted enclosures and sometimes they have added lighting. A sheltered space is needed where an audience can be seated, perhaps on a grassy bank or stone

steps, to watch and participate. Much less formal arrangements can be made for the pupils to enjoy the benefits derived from drama, through, for example, role play, self expression and mime. At a nursery school visited, the celebration of the Chinese New Year provided an opportunity for the children to fabricate Chinese artifacts, make face masks and together to construct a dragon. The children ate Chinese food which they had helped to prepare. Some dressed up in the dragon, and in the nursery grounds they re-enacted a Chinese play they had seen on television or had

Preparation of a video can be more relevant and rewarding in an outdoor setting.

witnessed in Chinatown. Schools have also been host to Mummers, to Morrismen and to street theatre groups who make use of the outdoor spaces to display their skills to the children.

1.15 Art

A wealth of experiences in Art can be provided on even the most limited school site. Indeed Art can be a stimulus for developing the grounds. Pupils, staff, and parents, through the need to broaden the quality of the environment, can develop their own sensory awareness and creative skills.

Grounds can give opportunities for the expressive visual representation of a pupil's emotions and ideas, as a response to what has been seen. This may be through drawing, painting, printing, photography, sculpture or modelling, perhaps using material developed or produced in the grounds. The school and its grounds can provide for observation and judgement and the development of manipulative skills through a variety of media. These might include pencil, chalk, charcoal, paint and dyes, some of which may be derived from the grounds.

Pavement art is yet another use of the tarmac playground – as a canvas for the whole class.

10

1.16 Music

Music skills can be developed outside. Natural or recycled materials can be used to make simple musical instruments, including drums and percussion instruments, reeds and pipes. It is possible to record sounds heard in the grounds and achieve the beginnings of simple musical notation. Singing and music making can be novel and exciting in the outdoor environment. They might derive from a study of folklore, religious festivals or 'stately' occasions.

1.17 Pupils with special needs

All pupils can benefit greatly from work outside and pupils with learning difficulties gain particular advantage from outdoor practical experiences, which provide relevance to their work that may be difficult to replicate in a classroom. Some of those who are not physically disabled but have learning difficulties have been found to gain confidence, learn well and become more settled through working in the outdoor environment. Experiences with animals, particularly larger livestock, have proved to have a therapeutic effect upon children with emotional and behaviourial difficulties. Involvement in active learning through observation and participation and in design and change in the grounds are particularly effective activities with these pupils. A first principle in providing for those with physically disabilities concerns access, and this affects the design of the spaces, paths, pond-sides, entrances and structures such as hides. For example, raised beds for planting out specimens and studying their growth would be useful for those in wheelchairs. At one centre for the physically disabled, ramps, suitably fitted with raised edges, extend into the pond to allow students in wheelchairs closer access to the water's edge.

Providing opportunities in the outdoor environment for pupils with disabilities has considerable implications for design, but the solutions to the problems posed must not deny those challenges that are the right of all pupils. It is not appropriate to provide undue help and guidance to pupils with disabilities; they need to learn through their successes and mistakes like everyone else.

1.18 Gifted children

In a discussion paper on gifted children in comprehensive schools, HMI[1] recommended that the science which is taught needs to be of an investigative nature; that able pupils should be given access to suitable resources; and that they need enriching experiences. In the same document it was suggested that gifted children studying geography should undertake wide-ranging investigations using a spread of resources including equipment for measuring and recording in the field. The grounds can be used to extend the learning experiences of pupils identified as highly gifted across a range of curriculum areas.

1.19 Other uses of the grounds

Up to 28% of a child's time in school (for example, before and after lessons, during breaks) can be spent in the school grounds. The nature of the grounds will have a profound effect upon what goes on during that time. Much will also depend upon the attitude of the school staff and the school's policies for the management of people and spaces during these times. The school is obliged to provide supervision but, for a variety of reasons, this is not always undertaken by qualified teachers. The possibility of there being inexperienced supervision means that special

Playground features can provide settings for drama and informal play.

Informal play between partners is best in a backwater, away from more boisterous games.

[1] DES HMI Series: *Matters for discussion 4: Gifted children in middle and comprehensive secondary schools.*

12

consideration needs to be given to planning and locating play activities.

During this time – often referred to as 'playtime' – children are free, within certain limits imposed by the school, to choose what they do. Children learn through play; it gives them opportunities to explore their own capabilities and their limitations. Through the medium of play they learn about themselves and other people. By trial and error, imitating others, practice and refinement, they develop a range of physical and social skills. They begin to understand social customs, the properties of a range of natural materials and artificial objects found in their environment. They learn to judge size, speed, distance, height, depth and width. They appreciate the benefits derived from caring and sharing, and the consequences of non-cooperation and selfishness. They have opportunities to develop and exercise their imagination.

Young children are curious and like to explore their environment. They may be attracted to sloping ground, mounds, hiding places, trees, and climbing equipment. They love to fantasise, to build, to dismantle and sometimes to destroy. As they develop, children indulge in more formalised play which demands regular patterns of behaviour and compliance with rules – some initiated from outside, some self-imposed. Later play may become ritualised and peer group led. Team and individual activities, including ball games, become a means for achieving success, impressing friends and self-testing, as

well as fun. Elements of drama and social exchange provide opportunities to develop associations and friendships, to handle disappointment and failure, to control anger and to cope with grief.

Many pupils like to play traditional ball games according to season and may dominate the asphalt playground to the disbenefit of others, especially where space is scarce. Statistics show that most accidents occur in the large unrelieved wide open playground through falls and collisions. Boisterous games have their place, but they should be contained and other areas should be provided for those who may have no interest in traditional team games. A variety of spaces should be created. There is a need for sheltered places with seating where children can meet in twos and threes to talk and listen, to exchange views and to sit quietly. There need to be places where a child can be alone to

There should always be an opportunity for quiet reflection.

Constructive play, such as this den building, requires a wild area with raw materials and sympathetic supervision.

The designation of a skipping corner is a simple and effective means of zoning play activities.

13

think. For older pupils especially, there is a need for a campus style of design, with spaces of different qualities and sizes, well endowed with site furniture for meetings and gatherings. Clearly the challenge is to achieve lively and varied external detailing whilst successfully providing for robust and heavy usage.

There are rich opportunities for study and the consolidation of learning, in addition to play, when playground markings provide for a traditional game like Hopscotch, or mathematical games which include logic tracks and problem solving patterns. Some board games can be adapted for the playground. There is a large range of play apparatus available from manufacturers who comply with the British Standards Institution recommendations.

If the grounds are designed to be an environment for learning, there will be many instances of pupils experimenting independently with equipment and ideas previously used in curriculum time, or continuing to pursue an investigation started in lesson time using the opportunities provided in the grounds for that purpose. To the participant this may be 'play' but the reinforcement of learning which is taking place and the new ideas which are being explored are important components of learning. Play is made up of self-chosen enjoyable experiences concerned with physical or social activities, both of which must be provided for. There is a need to allow

for a wide variety of activities which can go on at the same time in a number of different locations. These can be paved or grassed, can be sheltered by walls, trees, shrubs or a bank, or left relatively open.

Sometimes 'pump priming' of ideas from a teacher can lead to a new range of interesting pursuits for enthusiastic pupils. They may find all sorts of options to develop (often in most ingenious ways and with little equipment) from an activity introduced by the teacher as a simple game. Selected junk material is always useful – often more so than sophisticated single purpose manufactured playthings - for building and constructing imaginative creations of the children's own invention. Sometimes what teachers have observed happening in play can be put to good effect in the teaching programme.

1.20 Importance of different kinds and sizes of space

Study of many different school grounds has confirmed the importance of varied sizes and types of space, particularly for informal and incidental learning. Such space, if it is of high quality, can lead to a close and trusting relationship between the various users of the grounds and to respect for their local environment. The detailed nature of this landscape is examined more fully in Section 2.

Providing for Educational Use of Grounds: Qualities and Features

2.1 Landscape – a flexible resource

The school grounds are a potentially malleable resource that can be remoulded over time to meet the changing demands being placed upon them. The 'soft' landscape of grass, shrubs and trees is totally flexible. Only the more substantial elements of the 'hard' landscape, such as roads and car parking, and of course the buildings, mitigate against change. It is important to examine how this landscape might be harnessed to the general and specific educational needs discussed in Section 1 (Figure 1). Whilst there are differences in funding between new sites and existing grounds, the aims are essentially the same. It is wise to be aware of the practicalities on existing grounds, but not to restrict horizons unnecessarily. Emphasis must also be as much on longer term aftercare as on the initial implementation of change.

Large and healthy mature trees are an asset on any school site.

2.2 The setting

The local environment around a school is fundamental to educational use of its grounds. The appearance and activities of adjacent land-users must be reflected in the design and development of the grounds. They can, indeed should, contribute to its educational value. A view of the local scene costs nothing but it can say a great deal. Different neighbours and uses call for different responses in terms of their impact on both site layout and detailed boundary treatment. The challenge is to reflect the surrounding townscape or landscape in the broad pattern of site development, to the benefit of both school and local community. It may even be possible to use adjacent land – churchyard, park, wood or meadow – as an extension to the grounds and perhaps to afford resources that cannot be created within the site boundaries (Figures 2 and 3).

Every locality is in some way unique as a result of its geology, soils, landforms and vegetation. In the past human activities have worked with these natural factors rather than be imposed upon them. As a result, it is still possible to distinguish local variation in the character of the landscape and the built environment. The school site should express this individual identity rather than be renowned for its sameness or its dullness. The demands for breadth of opportunity and consequent resources in the grounds must be set alongside the need to convey a sense of belonging. In this respect it is important to remember that views are 'two-way', those into the school grounds being as relevant as those from them. Teachers and pupils can take the lead in assessing the visual qualities of their local environment as part of the curriculum in Art and Design.

FIGURE 1

NOTIONAL ARRANGEMENT OF OUTDOOR USES AND ACCESS

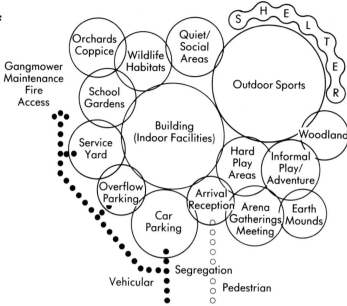

FIGURE 2

EDWALTON PRIMARY SCHOOL, NOTTINGHAM

Using adjoining woodland to develop a curriculum-related nature resource

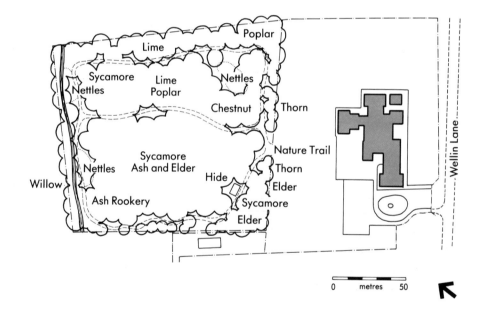

The school was built in the 1950s and is bounded by housing, a road and woodland. More recently it wished to extend the possibilities for outdoor study as the scope in its own grounds was limited. The use of the adjacent woodland was achieved with the help of the Rushcliffe Borough Council. The staff and pupils transformed the wood into a educational resource by organising the clearance of rubbish that had accumulated as the wood had been used as a dumping ground over the years. The Borough Council contributed to the expenses of the British Trust for Conservation volunteer workers who undertook those tasks that the school could not complete. The wood is now a resource for a whole range of curriculum activities: mapping, making tree surveys, monitoring tree disease, observing small mammals, studying insects, recording bird populations, and generally developing the reserve by tree management and planting, as well as caring for the fauna and flora. From time to time overnight camps are held in the wood and a replica saxon timber stockade has been created to commemorate the former settlement on the spot.

FIGURE 3

BARNWELL SECONDARY SCHOOL, STEVENAGE

A nature resource in a rectory garden

The grounds of an old rectory, which is part of the school grounds, forms the basis of a diverse educational resource. It allows for a wide range of activities and comprises an orchard, a copse, a hazel grove, a meadow, a pond and a bramble thicket. The whole of the area is interlaced with a meandering nature walk. Pupils have worked at enhancing the area themselves by putting in paths, clearing the pond and caring for the area in other ways.

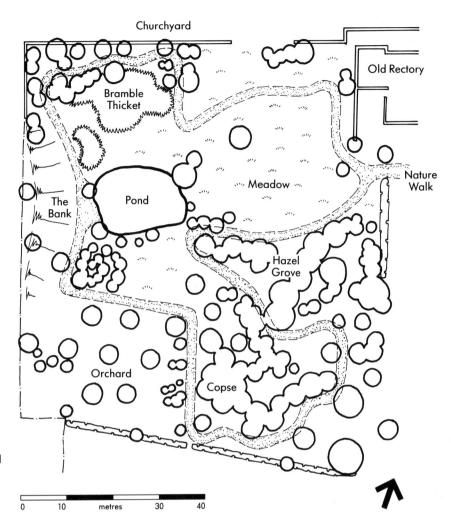

2.3 Boundaries

There can be no standard solution to boundaries, even around an individual school. They should be designed to reflect visual and practical use criteria and demand specific solutions that are both cohesive and effective in relation to the local environment and neighbouring uses (Figure 4). Boundaries send immediate messages about the school to pupils, parents and visitors. Chainlink on concrete posts rarely achieves either visual or functional objectives. There is a strong argument for the positive use of hedges wherever possible. These provide both a boundary and an educational resource. If robust activities, abuse or incompatible neighbours demand more substantial boundaries, such as weldmesh (ballstop fencing) or even

earth mounds, these can be softened by planting. With younger pupils, there is, of course, the vital question of their security in the grounds, which must influence the design of boundaries and gates. Problems of trespass and of dogs are as much an issue of site management as boundary treatment; and relate directly to the involvement of the local community. The condition and the nature of the site boundaries reflect the image of the school and depend as much on good management as on sound design.

17

FIGURE 4

FENCING AND ENCLOSURE
(numbered in order of cost)

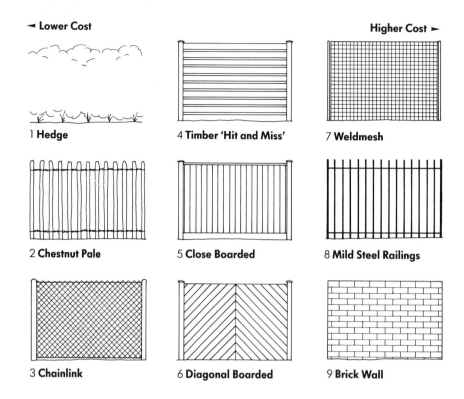

◄ Lower Cost   Higher Cost ►

1 **Hedge**   4 **Timber 'Hit and Miss'**   7 **Weldmesh**

2 **Chestnut Pale**   5 **Close Boarded**   8 **Mild Steel Railings**

3 **Chainlink**   6 **Diagonal Boarded**   9 **Brick Wall**

2.4 Sensory qualities

The school grounds should appeal to the senses of sight, sound, smell and touch and should be able to cope with a range of personal preferences for enclosed and open spaces, for active and passive uses, and for formal, structured and 'wild' unstructured areas. In order to satisfy educational requirements, it is important not to determine what will happen in every part of the site but to create a varied and flexible landscape that will afford many opportunities, some expected, others not even envisaged. The school grounds should be ever changing not static, stimulating not boring, welcoming not hostile, varied not bland. Although the reaction of visitors and the attitudes of neighbours are important, they should not predominate, but rather be reflected in the pattern of educational uses. Provided there is a landscape structure to create maturity and setting, change can be dynamic and ongoing, even to the extent of undoing or redoing earlier initiatives. The school building, its style, the materials from which it is built and its appearance all contribute towards the development of pupils' ideas and ideals about architectural quality and sense of place.

There is an immediate need on many school sites to create contrasting spaces of varying sizes and qualities which can appeal to different individuals and accommodate different uses. Given the sense of open space invariably conveyed by sports pitches, emphasis elsewhere can be on varying degrees of enclosure – the amphitheatre, the dell, the glade, the jungle or the outdoor room – with complete visual barriers, filtered glimpses and open views. These can afford potential for separation of active pursuits, such as ball games or chasing, and passive activities for groups, such as chatting, and for individuals, such as reading or reflecting. The way these spaces are linked is equally important in extending the range of educational opportunity. Their arrangement can afford a changing collage of experiences that create intrigue, anticipation and surprise (Figure 5). There is opportunity for teachers and pupils to be involved in sensory appraisal of their site and in developing ideas to enhance its character and qualities.

Where younger pupils have put forward their own suggestions as part of a wider consultation exercise, they are both revealing and significant. For example:

○ A place for adventure where we can make up our own games
○ A place for reading
○ A place to watch birds and other living things
○ An area for conversations
○ Places to hide
○ A frightening place
○ A place where we can be quiet
○ A place where we can build things

The essential feature is that both teachers and pupils are seeking variety and quality of space with a suitable ambience and usefulness, which does not necessarily mean the provision of expensive artifacts or surfaces.

2.5 Microclimate and pollution

Both the school buildings and the school landscape should seek to work with natural elements rather than defy them. The location of the building complex, its level in relation to its surroundings, its configuration and its orientation all have a major influence on microclimate. Teachers and pupils can take the lead by observing, recording and analysing local weather patterns. They can then design and implement measures to mitigate climatic extremes and thereby conserve energy indoors and assist greater use outside.

Even on an existing school site much can be done to overcome exposure and wind funnelling between buildings by shelter-belt planting. It is not just the buildings that require shelter, it is equally important for outdoor classrooms, study or play areas and sports pitches. (Figures 6 and 7) Shelter-belts may vary from a dense hedgerow to a 20 metre wide woodland, but only wider, higher designs allowing about 40% filtration will combat winds and reduce the chill factor over a greater

FIGURE 5

USING TREES TO PROVIDE SHADE

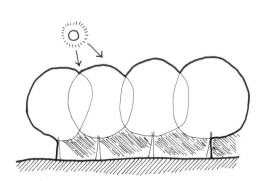

a)
A cool orchard or open woodland

b)
A mature standard tree provides shade

19

part of the site. Another advantage of shelter planting is the possible longer term savings on the building's energy budget. The benefit from shelter-belts often considerably outweighs any possible increase in heating demand due to shading. Since it is difficult to ensure all pupils wear appropriate clothing and footwear for outdoor activities, sheltered spaces and all-weather surfaces will do much to achieve all year round use.

Overhead elements, such as a roof canopy or the tracery of leaves formed by a tree's branches, create a sense of enclosure and refuge. They can also provide a large outdoor umbrella to give protection from the rain and form a shield from the sun. A large covered yard or even a small veranda is somewhere to sit or play, to feel secure from the rain pattering on the roof or the sun blazing down and yet to be part of an outdoor world rather than be confined to a building (Figure 8). It is another means of encouraging greater use throughout the year. Trees or even large shrubs are ideal sunshades but isolated specimens may attract excessive wear around their trunk. Retaining walls or circular seats might cope with the

problem but dispersion of wear by increased opportunities – an orchard for example – is a more attractive proposition.

Noise and air pollution are increasingly familiar obstacles to the use of the school site. Trees and shrubs are not successful in attenuating noise, which requires a solid barrier like a wall, fence or earth mound close to the source. At most they may achieve a psychological reduction by screening the noise source. They are more successful in filtering air pollutants, especially the finer leaved deciduous species and certain conifers. Such pollution screens would also create another educational resource. Walls and fences are high cost elements which offer an immediate screen and sound barrier and are valuable where space is restricted. Earth mounds or simple manipulation of site levels can achieve similar ends, by creating a steep, densely planted embankment facing the noise source and more gently sloping land within the site (Figure 9). It could be available for use by the school and might be modelled into a stage, terraces or ramps.

A belt of trees provides shelter, as well as being a feature and habitat in its own right.

Even large shrubs and quite small trees can create intimate shaded spaces for younger pupils.

The individual standard tree with dense foliage is a wonderful sunshade.

Log seats and grass in the shade beneath a large tree provide a unique and attractive setting for lunch-breaks.

The link between inside and outdoors is stronger with glazed halls and atria.

This enclosed space or 'shell' is ideal as both teaching and recreation space.

FIGURE 6

USING TREES TO PROVIDE SHELTER

Shelter-belts must allow some wind through them (ideally 40%) and they can reduce its speed by as much as 60% over an area up to ten times the shelter-belt height to windward and thirty times to leeward.

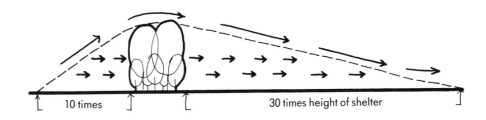

10 times   30 times height of shelter

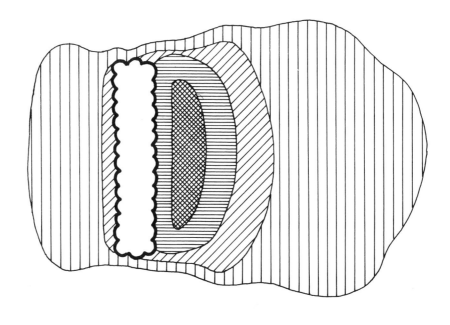

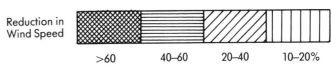

Reduction in Wind Speed

>60   40–60   20–40   10–20%

21

FIGURE 7

**CRESTWOOD
SECONDARY
SCHOOL,
EASTLEIGH**

**Sheltered school
parkland**

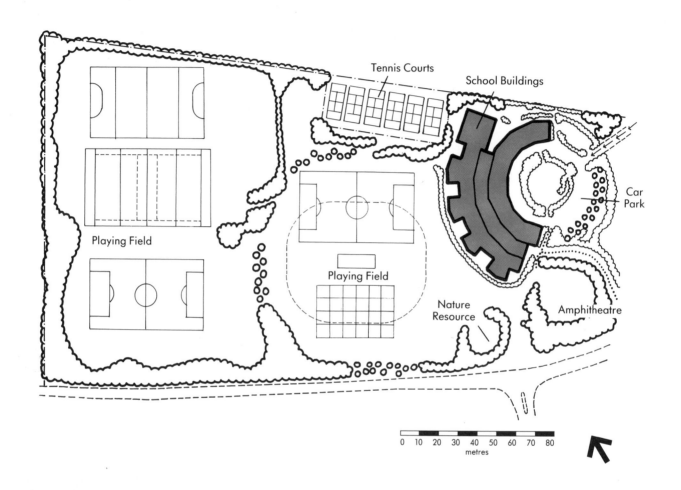

The landscape brief on this relatively new site was to create a sheltered environment with a range of different sized spaces for educational use and thereby parallel and continue the design concept established in the architecture of the school. Grounds provision was based around a framework of tree planting to modify the worst of the weather for those pupils involved in sporting and outdoor activities.

The requirement was for winter and summer games pitches, hard surfaced games courts, an amphitheatre for events, a conservation area to contain a pond and wetlands, and smaller enclosed and sheltered areas for quiet reading and leisure.

To realise these ideas, existing trees and hedgerows were retained and reinforced with new planting. In other areas tree planting and shelter-belts were introduced. A differential mowing regime created diversity, with the grass sward and distinguished between different uses.

The resulting overall school campus environment, inside and outside, gives a strong sense of enclosure, variety, and excitement in moving from one space to another.

FIGURE 8

CRESTWOOD SECONDARY SCHOOL, EASTLEIGH – THE 'STREET'

This simple concept creates an indoor/outdoor protected recreation space which can be used in breaks and after school. All the school facilities flank either side of the glazed roofed 'street'. The original thought was that the school 'street' should form a piece of urban fabric by providing a pedestrian link between the new housing and shopping area. Although for the present the 'street' is entirely used by the school, the potential remains for a public link.

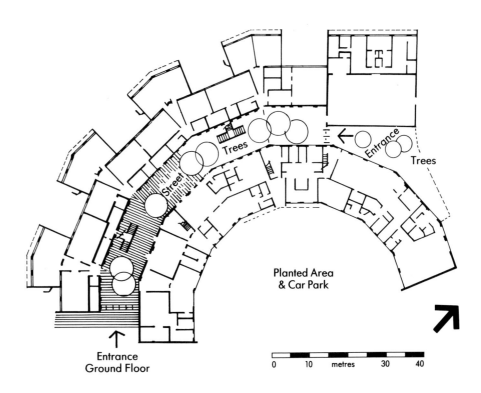

Trees

Entrance

Trees

Street

Planted Area & Car Park

Entrance
Ground Floor

0   10   metres   30   40

FIGURE 9

USING TREES AND EARTH MODELLING TO SCREEN OUT POLLUTION

Trees can filter dust but are far less successful in reducing noise

A combination of modelling and planting can reduce impact of traffic from above (d) below (c) or at grade (b).

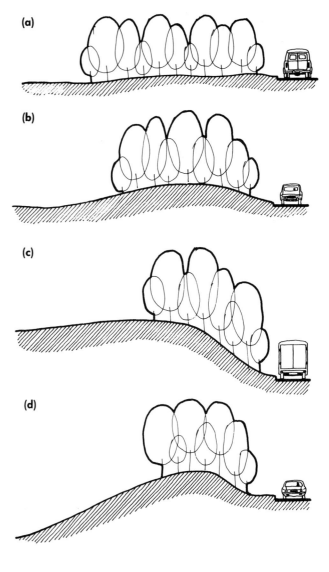

(a)

(b)

(c)

(d)

23

2.6 | Access and circulation

The main entrance to the school should be obvious and welcoming without the need for extensive signposting. Both hard surfaces and planting can be used to identify routes, which might be as bold and formal as an avenue of trees. Car parking should not dominate the school grounds in terms of either location or detailed design treatment. Change of level, earth modelling or a combination of the two offer the potential for immediate containment which, if reinforced by substantial planting, would also create summer shade. Internal walls or fences are alternatives which might save some space but these are generally more expensive. There is a greater argument for their use where they are dual purpose, as for example in the creation of a walled garden. Detailed design of the car park needs to cater for car overhang and doors opening by reducing the standard 5 metre bay and forming a 600 mm wide hard edge detail above the kerb.

Access has two distinct elements – pedestrian and vehicular (staff, visitors and service) – and positive segregation is vital on both aesthetic and safety grounds. Road access for fire appliances will be necessary, and the Chief Fire Officer should always be consulted early in the planning stage of building projects about fire fighting facilities. Where large numbers of pupils are likely to arrive by bike, they should be

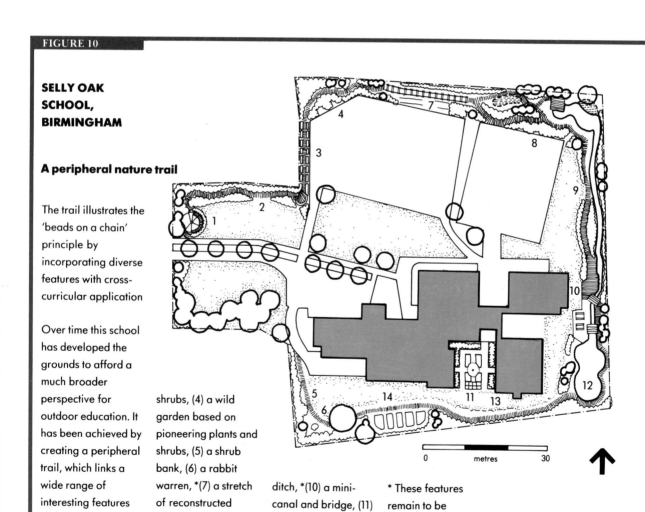

FIGURE 10

SELLY OAK SCHOOL, BIRMINGHAM

A peripheral nature trail

The trail illustrates the 'beads on a chain' principle by incorporating diverse features with cross-curricular application

Over time this school has developed the grounds to afford a much broader perspective for outdoor education. It has been achieved by creating a peripheral trail, which links a wide range of interesting features and incidents. These include: (1) a hornbeam sheltered sitting area, (2) an oak-ash woodland belt, (3) a reserve for scented and fruiting shrubs, (4) a wild garden based on pioneering plants and shrubs, (5) a shrub bank, (6) a rabbit warren, *(7) a stretch of reconstructed limestone ballasted railway track and signal from the Birmingham Urban Railway, *(8) a wild pond and wetland, *(9) an ecological ditch, *(10) a mini-canal and bridge, (11) a herb and vegetable garden, (12) a formal pond, (13) a bridleway to demonstrate rural crafts, and (14) a tree nursery.

* These features remain to be implemented.

0 metres 30

separated from other vehicles and suitable storage should be provided in secure areas such as a locked compound that is frequently overlooked. Segregation of pedestrians should equally aim to achieve not merely spatial division right from the entrance, but should, wherever possible, be separated from the road by modelling and planting. In the same vein, positive provision could be made in primary schools for parents at the beginning and end of the school day by inviting them onto the school site to sit or chat in a pleasant, restful space that affords some covered shelter. Since there is rarely a conflict in time, such provision could have a multi-use function as a social play area, outdoor classroom or arena.

Where there is a need for a number of pedestrian access points it is usually better to provide positively for them and to manage the site to ensure such access is not abused. Separate pedestrian entrances are another means of achieving segregation and may well preclude damage to boundaries and creation of 'desire lines', or natural routes. They could be researched, designed and used by pupils whilst being available to parents and the wider community. These footpath links might also be incorporated into a matrix of routes and trails across the site. Such linear features are most efficient in their use of space and can be designed to offer an ever-changing kaleidoscope of experiences. There could be a hierarchy of routes, some hard surfaced with tarmac, paving slabs or self-binding gravel, others defined by close-mown paths meandering through meadow, or wooden plank walks over wetlands (Figure 10). Full consideration of the needs of all who use the grounds should be given; these include pupils with disabilities, parents and visitors. The width of paths must also cater for groups of pupils, requiring 3 metres in some cases, and the direction must be the most natural, with an absence of sharp corners and the creation of larger areas around entrances where pupils gather.

2.7 Hard landscape

Roads, turning areas, lay-bys, parking bays, footpaths, patios, hard play areas and sitting areas demand individual hard surface detailing to create a rich diversity of materials, colours, shapes, textures, patterns and sizes (Figure 11). The challenge is to achieve these ends within both the budget and the brief so as to maximise the potential for educational use, yet

---

FIGURE 11

SURFACE TEXTURES AND PATTERNS

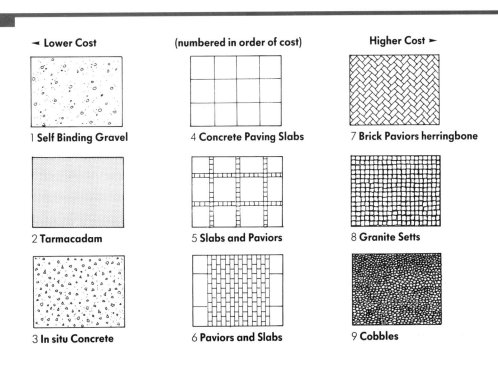

◄ Lower Cost   (numbered in order of cost)   Higher Cost ►

1 Self Binding Gravel   4 Concrete Paving Slabs   7 Brick Paviors herringbone

2 Tarmacadam   5 Slabs and Paviors   8 Granite Setts

3 In situ Concrete   6 Paviors and Slabs   9 Cobbles

not to appear like an exhibition of building materials. Even simple tarmacadam offers different size or colour of aggregate by means of surface dressing or pigment. Resurfacing work allows existing schools to take advantage of this flexibility. Indeed it is valuable if the hard surface detailing distinguishes between different uses on both amenity and safety grounds. Concrete and clay paviors and small element paving slabs have substantially extended the range of choice. Such high cost surfaces should not, however, be introduced at the expense of impoverishing the soft landscape around the site.

Tarmac has been adopted by practice and convention as an expedient hard-wearing surface for school playgrounds. It is usually marked out for a variety of play features for younger pupils and sporting activities for older pupils (Figure 12). Yet there is no reason why the tarmacadam area must be rectangular; an irregular, flowing outline containing the court(s) will create bays for informal play (Figure 13). Nor do two courts need to abut one another, especially in primary schools, although teachers may need a line of sight for observation of both for teaching and supervision purposes. Pitches set at angles to the boundaries offer opportunities for other activities, including nature resources (Figure 14). Whilst division of play areas requires astute detailing, the use of rebound walls and bays for seating, with related tree/shrub planters, can allow different uses on the separate areas and reduce the scale and impact of tarmacadam. At the secondary level there is often a demand for team games that require two or more netball-sized courts as multi-games areas. Where such hard surfaces have been constructed primarily for sports use, it is essential to allow separate provision for informal kick-abouts, gatherings or overflow parking so that the quality of surface is maintained.

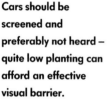

Cars should be screened and preferably not heard – quite low planting can afford an effective visual barrier.

The recent introduction of small element paving slabs now makes such marking-out of a chessboard on paving slabs unnecessary.

Bike stores are often forgotten; siting in a visible, 'self-policed' space is essential.

Walks around the periphery of the grounds make excellent use of space, but regular foot traffic demands hard surfacing.

Playground markings have educational as well as play uses, but surface materials must be suitable.

Marking-out of large features on the playground demands a suitable surface like tarmac.

FIGURE 12

COOMBES COUNTY INFANT SCHOOL, ARBORFIELD CROSS, READING

Playground markings, features and setting

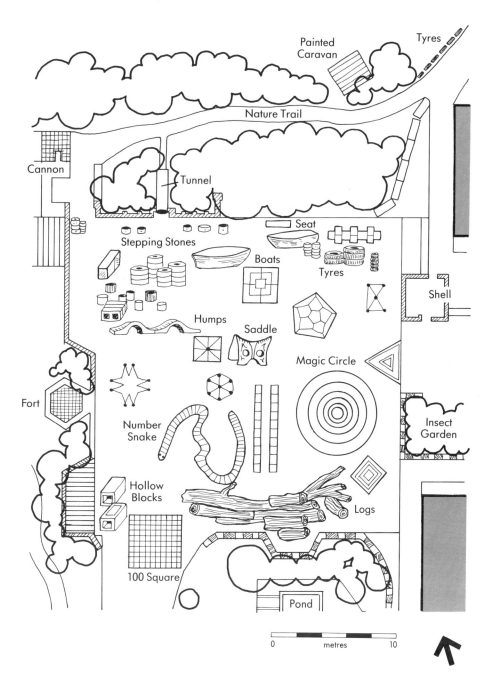

Labels in figure: Painted Caravan, Tyres, Nature Trail, Cannon, Tunnel, Seat, Stepping Stones, Boats, Tyres, Shell, Humps, Saddle, Magic Circle, Fort, Number Snake, Insect Garden, Hollow Blocks, Logs, 100 Square, Pond, 0 metres 10

In this example, all curriculum areas are served by using the grounds as a setting or reference for study, particularly that of mathematics, science, language, history and social education. There has been an attempt in the playground, as elsewhere in the grounds, to provide opportunity for learning through contrast and variety of experience. Skills learnt in the classroom can be practised out of doors and vice versa. The playground is principally a forum and theatre for school gatherings, spectacles and demonstrations. It is a place for organised teacher-led games and activities which can be reinforced and extended by the use of marking. There are painted markings in different colours on an asphalt surface. They are specially set out to define and to subdivide space into areas and shapes and there is provision for chess, hopscotch, snakes and ladders, the numbered grid, and the Schlegel mathematical figure. Other diamgrams stimulate thought, social interaction and games or relate to specific curriculum subjects – a compass and a clock. For children's play, this whole range of playground markings is available, together with further options – the 'Big foot', a chain of islands, the Zig Zag, the Spiral, and flow diagrams of chance and choice. These markings are reinforced by other features for play, such as fixed tyres to climb on, a boat, a concrete humpbacked bridge, the concrete saddle and shelter.

The playground boundaries offer other opportunities – a log pile and dwarf walls to climb on or to sit on. There are forts, tunnels, steps, a refuge and a multi-purpose sand pit which can double as a barbecue area.

For informal groups of two, three or more, there are 'shells', protected enclaves for story telling or for informal gatherings. The playground is the hub of the grounds and the outdoor heart of the school.

27

FIGURE 13

INFORMAL SHAPES OF TARMAC AND MOWN GRASS

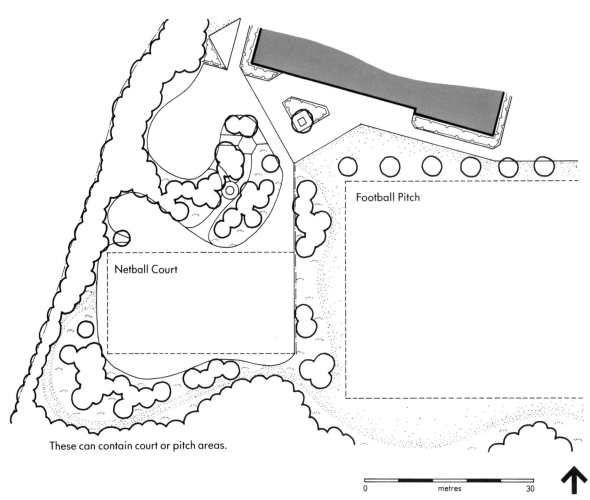

Netball Court

Football Pitch

These can contain court or pitch areas.

0   metres   30

FIGURE 14

PITCHES AT AN ANGLE TO SITE BOUNDARIES

create more viable spaces for other uses or activities

2.8 Site furniture and enclosure

Site furniture is a broad category that is too often narrowly interpreted in the design of external spaces. It usually means seats and more rarely applies to tables or worktops, litter bins, lighting, fences, trellises, pergolas, archways, hides or huts. There needs to be co-ordination and cohesion in such provision to avoid, for example, bollard lights being placed in shrub borders that will soon engulf them as plants mature. The three-dimensional elements can divide areas of varying character, create more space by taking the garden up into the air and be attractive in their own right. There is a clear requirement and evident demand on many school sites for more seating. This is more than just a question of benches on the edge of playgrounds, and must be related to small spaces and niches of varying character and quality. In social areas such provision might allow for cooking and eating outdoors, the picnic tables and benches also providing surfaces for drawing or writing. If properly designed and located, even a low retaining wall or a brick planter can function as a seat. The different demands and pressures between primary and secondary schools must be positively addressed in design terms.

Play equipment may be a proprietary product, an acquired artifact, such as a boat, or a do-it-yourself construction. It is often not provided as part of the capital budget and is inevitably most successful when developed subsequently in partnership with teachers and pupils. In either case it is essential for safety to foresee the likely zoning and pattern of uses and to create spaces and surfaces accordingly. At the same time it is important to maximise incidental play or social opportunities in the form of ball walls, retaining walls for sitting, earth mounds, sunken or quiet areas, slopes or ramps, covered yards or verandas (Figure 12). Play equipment may also be mobile in the form of tents, movable logs, timber, bricks, tyres, wheeled toys, bean bags or carpets. They require suitable space for both use and storage.

Clusters of seats away from the main playground are more conducive to informal play.

Sheltered sitting areas close to wildlife habitats present social and further educational opportunities at break times.

A low retaining wall around a standard tree provides both protection and seating.

Walls and picnic tables in small spaces created by planting allow a variety of different uses.

A large log forms a simple seat, but such sustained use requires a surrounding surface of bark or gravel.

2.9 ## Soft landscape and pressure of use

Mud is too often a common feature on existing school grounds, wherever the soft landscape of grass or shrub borders has been unable to sustain the intensity of use. In many cases perceived and actual pressures on the grounds, especially around the buildings, have been very different. This is seldom a result of indiscriminate or by any means undue patterns of use, nor of poor site management. It is more frequently a basic failure in the original design or expansion of the school, without accompanying investment in improvements to the grounds. Heavy and robust usage, particularly at the secondary level, must be provided for in site layout. Large congregation areas, wide paths, curved or 45° alignments, changes of level and appropriate edge details must all be considered. There should be no doubt that soft landscape areas will not merely survive, but positively thrive.

Mown paths amidst meadow may be all that is necessary in less frequently used areas.

Contrasting hard surfaces and earth modelling create an ideal arena for community events.

Clearly it is not possible to get everything right at the outset of new developments, and some resources should be available to deal with unforeseen 'desire lines' or other pressure points after patterns of use have been established.

2.10 Earth modelling

Before looking at the diverse range of vegetation that can be created within the school grounds it is vital to be aware of the importance of earth modelling and soil management, especially on the new school site. Earth modelling involves sculpting the ground surface to create varied landforms that can accommodate a new mix of uses. Thus it is possible to create changes of level in the form of mounds, hollows, ridges, arenas, slopes, terraces, plateaux, hills and valleys. If such modelling achieves a balance between 'cut' and 'fill', so that no soils are imported or exported, it can be extremely cheap. If surplus soil from building footings can be utilised for earth modelling on site, it offers further potential cost saving. The operation of mowing machinery should influence consequent gradients, but not dictate them. Afforestation of steeper slopes is a viable and attractive alternative to mown grass that may also make savings on the maintenance budget in the longer term.

2.11 Soil management

Another temptation has been to apply a horticultural perspective to the stripping and placement of topsoil to promote maximum growth, whereas positive manipulation of soils can be used to create areas of overburden and subsoil with impoverished conditions at the surface. It might even be possible to leave a natural soil profile, a sand or a rock face or simply examples of underlying rocks as a teaching resource. Impoverishment of soils will reduce grass growth and consequent mowing and enhance diversity of flora. Surplus topsoil can be used to improve the growing medium in woodlands, orchards or gardens. Such variety will feed the curriculum across a range of subjects.

2.12 Trees

Structure planting of native trees and shrubs takes time to establish and must be a priority on the school site so that pupils can soon walk under trees, kick leaves and have the feeling of being in woodland. Forestry transplants 300–600 mm in height, planted in random species groups of 1 to 10 in number and at 1.5–2 m apart, are ideally suited to the creation of small woodlands, copses or shelter-belts. They can be easily grown from seed or cuttings in the school nursery.

Earth modelling around the pitch provides a natural grandstand.

Grass terraces formed in a bank are ideal for large gatherings, provided grass mowing has been well planned.

31

Their growth is more rapid than larger nursery stock, often 300 mm or more per annum, and within 5 to 8 years they can make a meaningful contribution to the landscape. They are small enough for pupils to plant and sufficient in numbers for them to identify with individually. For more immediate impact, much larger, heavy standard trees 3.5–4.5 m high provide a more robust alternative especially suited to urban sites or areas close to heavy usage. Species choice for wildlife value is best based on those indigenous species common in the locality, although educational demands may include a variety of leaf shapes, colours and sizes, different forms of seed, buds, twigs, bark or blossom. This is an area where sound landscape advice is essential.

2.13 Hedges

Hedges usually require a simple agricultural fence with plain wire during their establishment phase, yet are still cheaper in capital terms than chainlink. An attractive option is a thorn mixture of 70–90%, enriched by 2– 4 occasional hedge species common in the locality. Once established the hedge can be cut regularly or be allowed to grow on and eventually laid in the traditional manner. If there are no neighbouring constraints, trees can be included as individuals or small groups in the hedgerow, thereby enhancing its landscape significance. There is no reason why hedges should be thought of merely as a boundary treatment. They may be used very effectively within the school grounds to separate

A diversity of plant canopies – groundcover, shrubs and trees – creates variety in landscape and habitat.

uses, to define spaces, to screen and to shelter. Beech, hornbeam, evergreen or other ornamental shrubs are alternatives to the thorn hedge in these situations.

2.14 Scrub

Another vegetation type worthy of consideration is scrub, typical of unmanaged grassland which over a period of 10 to 15 years has been colonised by a variety of shrubs and trees set randomly in groups and in isolation. Scrub growth amongst meadows with pathways mown through would satisfy a frequent demand by teachers and pupils to 'roughen the site up!' There is, however, a danger that the pendulum will swing from the extreme of horticultural delight to that of ecological correctness with regard to choice of species. In truth the grounds present the potential for a more artistic and horticultural approach, perhaps closer to the buildings, merging gradually into a more 'natural' and sylvicultural theme towards the periphery. There is no reason why the former cannot be designed to be of value for wildlife or the latter to provide visual delight.

Rather than burn logs and branches, a range of habitats can be created with them.

The ability to search or hide amongst woodland is often a missing ingredient in school grounds.

This close study of birch bark highlights the need to plan for, and allow, robust investigation.

Sowing a wildflower meadow can be organised from the outset as a school project.

Planting wildflowers raised from seed is a viable alternative to sowing, especially where the existing ground flora is to be retained.

Climbers, used in this case to form a unique school entrance, are often a neglected resource, especially where space is restricted.

2.15 Shrub borders

There has been a tendency to use shrub borders for residual spaces or where windows open outwards. A low sill then demands constant pruning of shrubs beneath the windows to restrict height and maintain light, in which case they are rarely visible from the classroom. They are at the same time prone to wear from adjacent, heavily used footpaths. That is not to say that shrub borders should not be sited against buildings, rather that the design and use objectives must be clear and a suitable growing environment created. They generally need to be at least 1.5 metres wide and well away from the roof overhang.

Special edge treatment or change of level is necessary near to doorways, paths and other areas of heavy usage. Shrub borders can be as expensive to establish as cheap hard surfaces. Their maintenance costs are also relatively high, if done properly, which argues for their being used judiciously and for a purpose. It might be to clothe a blank wall, for visual delight, to form a herb garden or herbaceous plants for cut flowers, to shelter, screen or define external spaces, or, most importantly, to attract birds and insects right up to the classroom window for observation by the pupils.

Monitoring wildflower establishment affords educational opportunities across the age range and throughout the curriculum.

I hear and I forget,
I read and I remember,
I do and I truly understand.

2.16 Bulbs

For the price of one heavy standard tree it is possible to purchase five hundred bulbs, so creating a magnificent drift of flowers that may continue to multiply and vividly herald the optimism of a coming spring. Bulbs and corms have been a neglected aspect of the soft landscape on the school site. Frustrations to the mowing regime can be overcome by siting a spring meadow around and beneath groups of trees, thereby also restricting the danger of mower damage to trees. This is another case where teachers and pupils can take on responsibility for planting and with it a sense of involvement and ownership.

2.17 Lawns and wild flower meadows

Increasing interest in wild flower meadows might immediately be met in certain areas by allowing occasional breaks in the mowing regime on lawns, so that daisies, buttercups, speedwell or clover can flower. Variation in the mowing regime also presents the opportunity to break down the scale and monotony of close mown grass and to avoid rectangular shapes. In the same way that the netball court does not need to be sited on a rectangle of tarmac, so the pitch area(s) could be contained within flowing curves of longer grass or meadow. Positive enrichment or replacement of an existing sward by sowing or planting demands sound advice as to the site and the species. Successful techniques include turf transplants from a species-rich sward, using late-cut species-rich hay as a seed source, sowing a proprietary wild flower seed mixture or raising wild flowers from seed and setting them in

Differential mowing regimes create contrasting textures, colours and habitats and break down the scale of the grounds.

Where resources and supervision allow, learning often continues outside lesson time.

an existing sward as young plants. They all require close monitoring and careful management, both of which have direct curricular application, as indeed has the initial choice and variety of techniques used. It can be particularly attractive and useful if wild flowers are brought right up to the classroom windows. At the same time, it is important to make the grounds, especially near the buildings, appear loved and cared for. Close mowing of a single swathe width or larger area close to paths and hard surfaces is one means of achieving this. There could equally be a place for the formal, manicured lawn in courtyard or sheltered spaces to allow for croquet or outdoor bowls.

2.18 | Water

Water should always be considered as an integral part of the soft landscape since it affords a uniquely stimulating and attractive medium for teachers and pupils. Questions of safety must affect how and where water is used but they should not preclude it. Existing ponds, ditches and marsh land on new school sites should be retained wherever possible and appropriate. Clean surface water from hard surfaces could be directed to a wet meadow, marsh, or pond,

A hard edge to one side of a pond allows for congregation, dipping and sampling.

Soft edges to a pond are more natural, but often mean more difficult access and cannot sustain intensive use.

provided any surplus overflow is catered for. This might be by means of open ditches, thus creating a further rich resource, rather than hiding all water underground in pipes. Poorly draining soils in low-lying areas may only need to be scooped out to hold water, at least in winter. More permanent water areas may require a butyl liner, concrete or puddled clay. Study and observation demand specific and safe edge detailing in the form of paving slabs, timber decking or shelving gravel around a part of the pond. A raised pond is an attractive alternative, suited to use by pupils with disabilities, but less attractive to wildlife if it is completely enclosed, and it is more expensive.

2.19 Crops

It has already been seen how the growing and observation of plants has applications across the curriculum. This can be far more than growing radishes or sunflowers, and may include all types of vegetable and garden flowers, cornfields, tree nurseries, orchards, soft fruit, hops, nutteries, osier beds or even coppice. They offer the means not merely to become directly involved in crop production but also to diversify and enrich the grounds. Broadening the potential for crop production on the

Orchard trees are multi-purpose – food source, landscape feature and sunshade.

Location close to the school has encouraged this dinner lady to help with bulb planting.

Planters allow the introduction of flowers to barren tarmac yards.

restricted area of the school site does not mean the omission of ornamental plants but rather a blending of the two. In some cases shrub borders have been successfully converted to crop production, thus bringing it right up to the classroom window. Alternatively, specific growing areas can be provided either as long, narrow strips or as family plots. Strips of cultivated ground are easier for the groundstaff to rotovate periodically and can be divided by rows of paving slabs to facilitate access.

Growing crops close to play areas may we require protection, bu they form an additional attraction for both participants and spectators.

2.20 Animals

The keeping of animals in the school grounds can involve both temporary and permanent provision and extend from a pet corner to a community farm. The creation of small enclosures in courtyards or the corner of a

Artificial habitats can also be a sculpture and landscape feature.

Pet hutches within a larger, secure enclosure afford greater freedom for animals and pupils.

A small paddock close to the school allows short visits from farm animals.

Erection of temporary fencing is another way of catering for animal visits.

building will allow pets or even small livestock to be kept during the day with great potential for observation and study. Similarly, to have a small paddock area where larger farm animals could be brought onto the site for a day or possibly longer would increase the range of opportunities.

2.21 Sports pitches

The provision of sports pitches has been the single most significant factor shaping the appearance and character of many school sites. It has been amply documented in *Building Bulletin 28* (along with recreation areas) and is the only outdoor resource that is subject to precise definition of space standards. Layout of pitches at an angle to site boundaries, rather than parallel to them, can create triangular pockets of land for other environmental resources that might focus on a specific educational aspect or subject and enhance the school setting. It also makes more space behind goals and still allows for moving pitches around

on the larger school site (Figure 14).

Recent research has revealed that natural grass pitches without improved drainage can sustain little more than three hours use per week during winter as against the seven hours prescribed in the Education (School Premises) Regulations. At the same time, advances in the construction of both natural and synthetic surfaces offer the opportunity to exceed these targets. There is a good argument for improving those pitches with the best location and qualities, and achieving more diverse usage on the remainder. Trim trails, assault courses, camping or other outdoor educational pursuits are all possible on pitch areas with poor potential for team games. Such diversification might include the creation of varied habitats for wildlife which would also form a setting for these outdoor activities.

On the new school site, it is vital that high specification construction and drainage techniques are used from the outset. Options for improving existing natural turf facilities range from introducing a drainage matrix of sand/gravel slits to completely replacing the rootzone with medium fine sand, possibly combined with the strategic use of reinforcement materials to help stabilise areas prone to intensive wear. Some of the cost of these improvements may be offset because they can then be used to generate a greater potential for shared use.

The DES and the Sports Council have jointly sponsored research into the construction, maintenance and use of natural turf winter games pitches. The monitoring of the use by players and the collecting of scientific data has been undertaken by the Soil Science Unit of the University College of Wales, Aberystwyth, and the Sports Turf Research Institute respectively. To date their findings from a small sample of specially constructed pitches representing the pitch construction types most widely used suggest the following in terms of hours of adult play per week during the winter months.

	Maximum adult usage per week
undrained pitches	
pipe drained pitches	3 hours
slit drained pitches with sand top dressing	6 hours
sand carpet pitches	9 hours
sand profile pitches with controllable water table	12 hours

The researchers estimate that a pitch's ability to sustain wear related to 8-16 aged pupil play would approximate to nearly double that of adult play.

The research indicates that regardless of construction types, usage and maintenance, guidelines must be strictly adhered to in order to prolong the life span of the facilities, maintain acceptable playing quality of the surface and reduce renovation costs. Undrained and pipe drained pitches will inevitably suffer from poor playing quality during and after heavy rainfall, and usage cannot be planned as accurately as with the other types of construction.

The establishment of young trees creates many tasks that can beneficially be performed by pupils.

Even where maintenance skills require external help, the educational potential of such work need not be lost.

When pupils take on care of the grounds it often leads to a sense of ownership and responsibility.

Moveover, the undrained and pipe drained pitches are more likely to become totally unusable if played on under adverse weather conditions.

2.22 Security

The school landscape must minimise the likelihood of wanton damage whilst ensuring a safe and secure environment for pupils and teachers. Security has been the subject of a DES publication[2] . The argument that management approaches should aim at ensuring the premises are, at all times, kept in a state of good repair and should encourage constructive and supportive attitudes amongst pupils, staff and parents is equally applicable to the grounds. 'There is seen to be a relationship between appearance, ethos and image of a school and the way it is perceived and treated both by pupils and the surrounding community.' Such a good housekeeping approach is considered to be the most cost-effective security measure. Moreover,

the grounds have more potential than the buildings for the pupils to become actively involved in care and development and thereby to assume a sense of ownership.

2.23 Safety

Thorny shrubs, uneven hard surfaces and broken fencing can all affect safety in the grounds, but it is surfaces beneath play equipment which have been the subject of most recent discussion. Yet the majority of playground accidents involve collisions and related falls on the same level, where overcrowding or poor layout of equipment may be contributory factors. This does not necessarily result from a lack of space, rather a lack of choice, the dearth of stimulating and interesting opportunities causing local crowding. Clearly, play equipment must never be dangerous, although it may only be attractive to pupils if it incorporates some risk. Indeed pupils may well create risk-taking situations where the play environment does not provide them. Impact absorbing surfaces that are available include sand, wood chips and bark, rubber tiles or shredded rubber, but they all require ongoing maintenance and only constant vigilance can minimise the risk of accidents. Supervision must be astute yet not restrictive, since the more dispersion of pupils that is allowed, the greater their opportunities for play and the less the problem of consequent wear, especially to the soft landscape.

2 Crime Prevention in Schools: Practical Guidance

Roles and Relationships

3.1 Potential participants

Achievement of any design or management initiatives to enhance the educational use of grounds is absolutely dependent on partnership and teamwork. Their disparate nature and the lack of a common purpose have been major impediments to progress in the past. Every local education authority is to some degree unique in the way in which care and development of the grounds are arranged. Yet the issues of close partnership between education and landscape staff, and within the latter group between designers and managers, relate to all of them. Those who could be involved are set out in Figure 15.

Whilst success can be achieved by one individual – and there are many examples of this – it is richer and more lasting where it involves teachers and pupils, educational advisers and landscape specialists. A 'whole school' approach can recognise mutual benefits, resolve conflict and overcome a notable reluctance, at all levels and even within the education service, to involve pupils right from the outset. There may well need to be a small working group and one member of staff taking on a liaison role for the grounds, especially as it relates to day-to-day maintenance. Communication is the key. Everyone must participate and if someone leaves the school there should always be two or three potential replacements. If there is a written policy commitment to educational use of the grounds by an individual school, and preferably by the LEA, it will provide a firm platform for newcomers to develop this role.

3.2 Diffusion of landscape skills

Personal qualities and informal working relationships have had more influence than organisational structures in determining the quality of the landscape service. In the hands of a sensitive landscape manager, attuned to the value of the school site educationally and environmentally, initiatives in the school grounds have flourished. The absence of such attitudes and teamwork has resulted in the adoption of traditional and essentially unchanging maintenance.

A major feature of all local authorities is that design and management of grounds are seldom unified. Location in quite separate departments is commonplace. Yet there is no clear distinction between the two roles in practice: designers influence the nature and type of management, and managers influence the establishment of a new landscape scheme. The achievement of educational objectives is totally

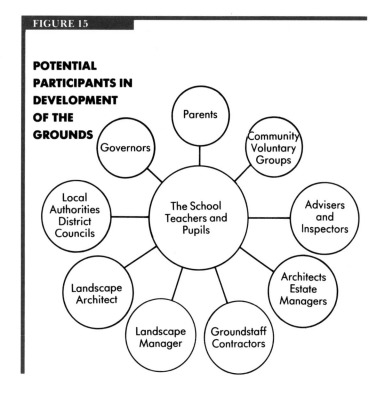

FIGURE 15

POTENTIAL PARTICIPANTS IN DEVELOPMENT OF THE GROUNDS

- Parents
- Community Voluntary Groups
- Governors
- Local Authorities District Councils
- The School Teachers and Pupils
- Advisers and Inspectors
- Landscape Architect
- Architects Estate Managers
- Landscape Manager
- Groundstaff Contractors

dependent on partnership between these interlinked disciplines. There is a strong argument for encouraging greater contact either by inter-departmental working teams or by secondment of staff. By such means, daily, as opposed to monthly or even yearly, contacts can be maintained.

3.3 An inter-disciplinary approach

The relationship between landscape and education staff is even more critical. As one teacher observed: 'It is generally felt that the schools themselves must have an active role in managing their sites. The problem is that no-one in education is trained to control standards of grounds maintenance. The Local Education Department is the client but often does not know what it wants and therefore allows grounds maintenance officers the dominant role in the process!' This isolation has been breaking down and it will be accelerated with the introduction of Local Management and the potential for greater participation by teachers and pupils.

Teachers plan and understand their own work but are not always aware of what they need from the school grounds or what they could quite easily have. Conversely, landscape architects and managers may not appreciate educational demands on the outdoor environment, which are often most ably expressed by pupils. There is much to be gained from the inter-disciplinary approach. Landscape staff could directly assist the education advisory service by showing schools how new outdoor resources can be created and maintained. Teaching staff and pupils could work with landscape managers to ensure the service is more directly tailored to the needs of the school. Such liaison must be co-ordinated so that schools always know whom to contact and for what advice or services.

3.4 Training

Greater benefits can also accrue if an inter-disciplinary approach is adopted towards training. Thus teachers could contribute to landscape training courses and landscape staff to educational courses. Indeed this could ultimately extend to courses by one discipline for the other. Only by this means can there be a fuller understanding of the constraints and opportunities, the means and the ends. It is another way of ensuring that designers, managers, educational advisers and teachers work in partnership on a daily basis.

3.5 Implementation

A school taking on sole responsibility for an area or landscape staff providing resources in isolation are both approaches prone to failure. The active type of learning demanded by the National Curriculum requires involvement leading to a sense of ownership. At the same time, extensive new works and aftercare may depend on specific technical skills, labour and machinery. A mixed economy, where the school identifies those tasks it can undertake to the educational benefit of the pupils and those for which it needs support from landscape staff, is likely to be most successful. It relies on the closest liaison and understanding between the school and the local landscape supervisor. He or she must exercise a light touch in supporting and advising teachers and pupils, frequently in the background but always available. It is a far more challenging, yet an infinitely more rewarding, role.

The degree to which a school may need such support depends on the age range of the children and the attitudes, skills and contacts of the teachers. Some teachers may have the ability, although not necessarily the time, to undertake much of the work in partnership with their pupils and merely require occasional logistical help in the form of labour, machinery or materials. Others may have useful contacts with local voluntary agencies or through the governing body. Consultation with parents, neighbours and the local community is also essential, and it may lead to offers of support and direct assistance. Such voluntary help is far more feasible for new works than for ongoing maintenance, since there is no long-term commitment. Greater emphasis on showing schools how they can do things for themselves and where they can get advice and material support can only further their direct involvement. Full participation by pupils throughout this process achieves educational objectives, such as skills in English, Mathematics and Design, together with learning in environmental and social education.

Design and Development

4.1 The new school site

Whilst the principles of landscape design and management to maximise educational opportunities can apply equally to new sites and existing grounds, their implementation takes place within totally different frameworks. New sites form part of a capital programme, where specific financial resources are allocated and there is a building team directly responsible for the works.

4.2 The brief

The development of the brief for a new school site is an evolutionary process. The landscape deserves as much attention as the building. It should never be standard or static since changing ideas and techniques merit experiment and evaluation for inclusion in future briefs. Beyond the need to state size of areas and number of facilities, it should explain the aims and aspirations of teachers and pupils and the character, qualities and features to be created for maximum educational opportunity. Design of the overall site layout and detailed landscape treatment demands guidance on their purpose. The adult perception of designed orderliness, colour, texture and scale is often different from that of the child and it is important to consult widely with teachers and pupils to create an outdoor environment that they will value and use. Since there should be no such thing as a 'standard' brief, emphasis must be on the approach and the areas it should cover, as outlined in Appendix 3.

4.3 Site selection

In the same vein, the choice of a greenfield site should include not just financial, land ownership and planning factors but also that of use potential. A flat featureless piece of land is ideal for convenience of building and playing field construction but hopeless for early establishment of a landscape framework. A site with diverse landform or extensive vegetation that relates well to the local community it serves may present design problems but it also provides character, challenge and opportunity. If these requirements can be fed into the local planning process early enough, they will reap rewards and overcome financial and ownership problems.

4.4 A site appraisal

It is important that all members of the building team should present the site's constraints and opportunities from the specialists' viewpoint. In landscape terms it may involve significant landform or existing vegetation, shelter or exposure, views from and to the site, soil conditions, implications of playing field construction, access, orientation and circulation (Figure 16). It makes sound sense to retain mature trees wherever possible rather than wait 30-60 years to replace them. It takes only a few hours to destroy what might have needed generations to establish. Existing overhead or underground services, planning requirements, easements, covenants or public rights of way are other issues which must be addressed at the outset. In order to meet future deadlines such details can be prepared by the landscape architect as soon as the site enters the building programme, and should always be available to the architect before any design work commences. It could take the form of a site appraisal which accompanies the brief or, where applicable, is incorporated within it. The documented history of the site, its past development and the related

FIGURE 16

LANDSCAPE APPRAISAL

(This has been simplified for publication purposes, and a detailed checklist is set out in Appendix 1)

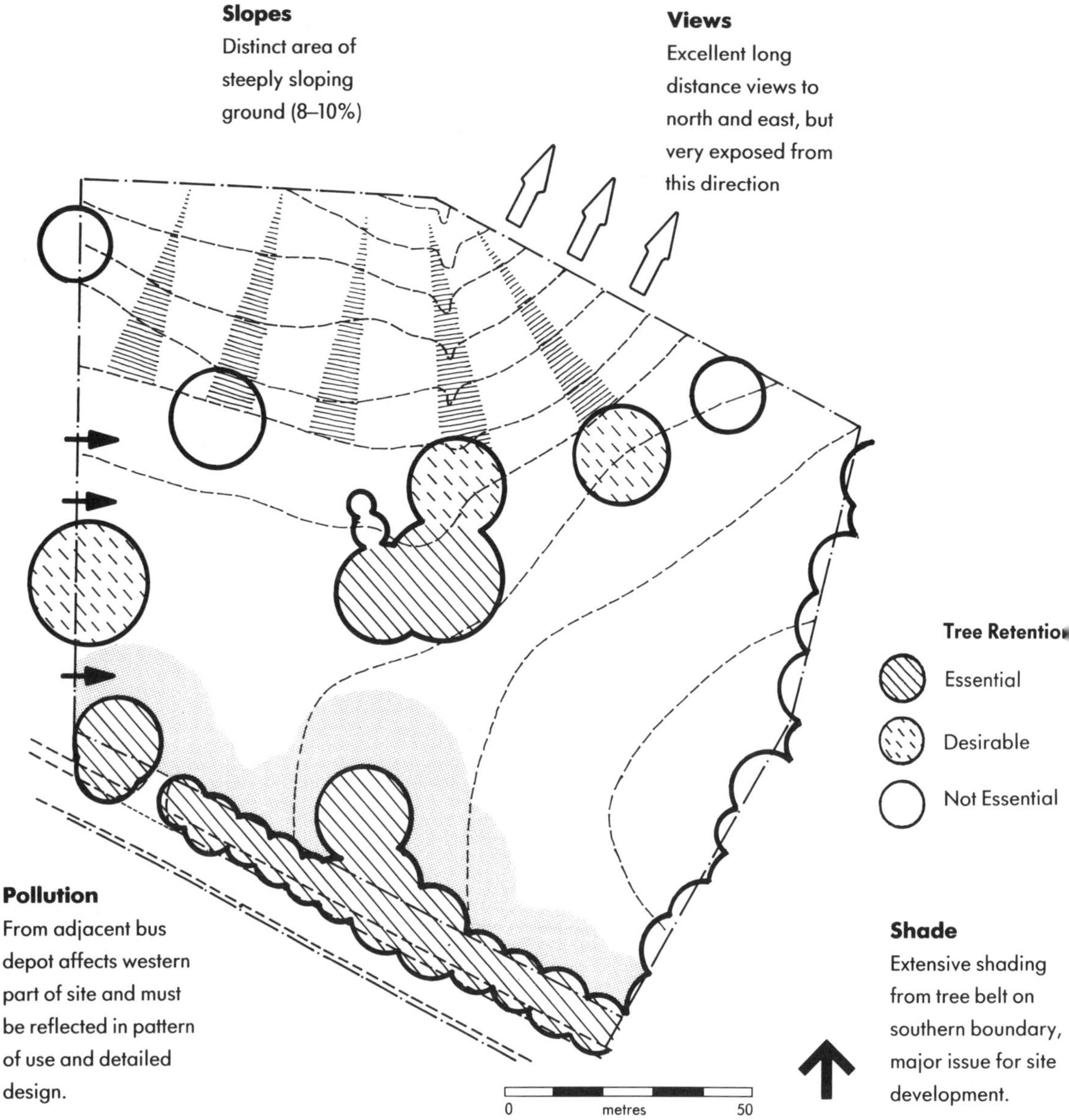

Slopes
Distinct area of steeply sloping ground (8–10%)

Views
Excellent long distance views to north and east, but very exposed from this direction

Tree Retention

⬤ Essential

⬤ Desirable

◯ Not Essential

Pollution
From adjacent bus depot affects western part of site and must be reflected in pattern of use and detailed design.

Shade
Extensive shading from tree belt on southern boundary, major issue for site development.

0 metres 50

reports and drawings will form the basis of useful indoor/outdoor class studies later on. It is important that copies of all these documents are made available to the school.

4.5 Options

Since the spatial disposition of the major elements on the site – location and relationship of building(s), playing fields access, servicing and parking, hard and grass play areas – are absolutely crucial to landscape and educational opportunities, it makes sound sense to be flexible and look at all the options. Two, three or more notional layouts, incorporating these main elements, may be feasible and

worthy of discussion and development with teachers and pupils (Figure 17). Design, management and use considerations will need to be placed in a financial context when appraising options but costs should not be the only selection criteria. In essence, the preferred option should look and work best. This stage should never be rushed since in landscape and educational terms the main issue is not the detailed treatment but the overall site layout. It is essential that substantive work on site is not undertaken until a preferred option is agreed, to avoid negating site features it might be possible to retain or develop.

FIGURE 17

**OPTIONS FOR
SITE
DEVELOPMENT**

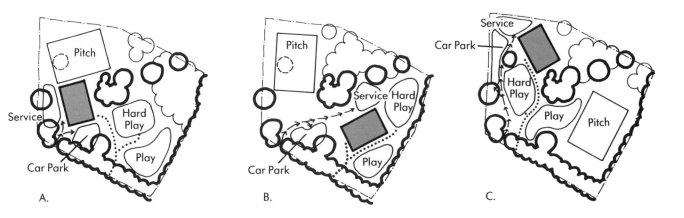

A.

B.

C.

4.6 Budget estimates

Once a site is included in the capital programme an overall cost needs to be established and it is often required before detailed site planning is undertaken. It is vital that the landscape architect prepare an outline estimate for external works at this stage for inclusion in the total project cost. Provided due allowance is made for the uniqueness of the individual site, such an estimate can be based on a simple elemental rate for the main components – sports facilities and playing fields, site furniture, boundary fencing, play and social areas, tree surgery and management, habitat creation, planting, seeding and aftercare (Figure 18). The last is especially important as Local Management means a global grounds maintenance budget is no longer available for each authority to cover establishment costs. Aftercare as part of capital works should include at least one year's maintenance for grass areas and three years' maintenance for planting areas.

FIGURE 18

**EXTERNAL
WORKS AS A
PROPORTION OF
TOTAL BUILDING
COSTS**

The proportion is usually between 10% and 20%, although it may be lower if playing fields are not included, and higher on difficult sites with abnormal costs.

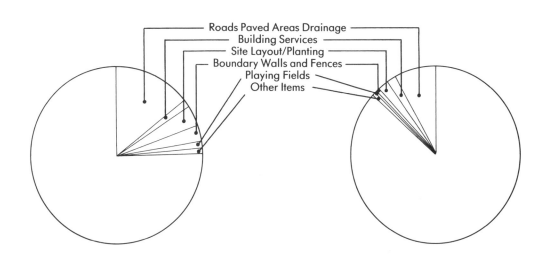

Roads Paved Areas Drainage
Building Services
Site Layout/Planting
Boundary Walls and Fences
Playing Fields
Other Items

4.7 Development of the landscape scheme

It is far preferable if the landscape details accompany the planning application and, as a result, the design of the site is developed in partnership with the architect. It gives both the client and the planning officer a much better indication of what the whole site should look like. Similar liaison should ensure that much of the landscape scheme can be implemented in tandem with building construction, provided individual contract areas and related access are clearly defined. It is then possible not only to create plateaux for playing field(s) but also to remodel any other parts of the site outside the building contract area. Unless future teaching staff are available for discussion, there is much to be said for creating several protected, partially screened spaces of varying size and character which could subsequently be developed by the school in liaison with their landscape advisers.

4.8 Advanced planting

By no means all of the site will require remodelling. Indeed there is advantage in retaining parts undisturbed, especially where planting is to be established. Trees and shrubs generally grow better and faster in such conditions, and, importantly, can be established at an early stage. Ideally, such advanced planting should take place a few years prior to building construction, so that these new landscape features have time to establish. The main obstacles to overcome are usually ownership and/or tenancy and funding, but every year that can be gained is a season's growth. At the very least it is essential to have the landscape budget approved so that all works outside the building contract area can proceed at the same time.

4.9 The landscape budget

The financial provision for external works, and for soft landscape in particular, should not be arbitrarily reduced as a result of overspending on the building. Whereas the building tender is a known sum at approval stage, landscape costs have usually been in the form of an estimate until building works are nearly complete. Thus the landscape estimate has sometimes been treated as a contingency sum, since finances have not been committed. This can be avoided by emphasis on advanced landscape works, by early and phased implementation of the rest of the scheme and by the fact that the design is curriculum based rather than simply cosmetic. It is neither desirable nor efficient to believe that external works are somehow less important and can be added at a late date. Indeed it is preferable if a small proportion of the landscape budget is retained to fund adjustments required

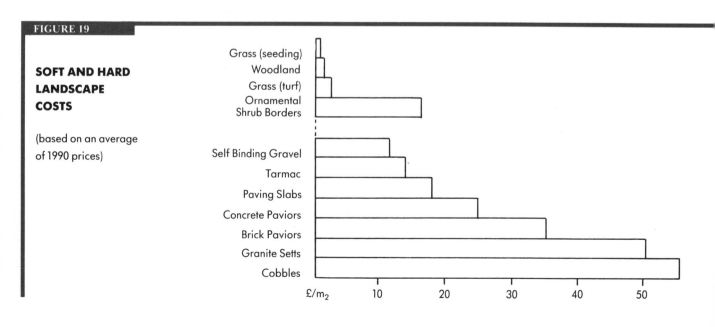

FIGURE 19

SOFT AND HARD LANDSCAPE COSTS

(based on an average of 1990 prices)

Grass (seeding)
Woodland
Grass (turf)
Ornamental Shrub Borders

Self Binding Gravel
Tarmac
Paving Slabs
Concrete Paviors
Brick Paviors
Granite Setts
Cobbles

£/m$_2$ 10   20   30   40   50

by the new users. Where funds are limited, it may be better to invest in earth modelling and extensive 'natural' planting, which help define space as major three-dimensional elements, rather than ornamental shrub borders or expensive paving details as an alternative to tarmac. (Figure 19)

4.10 Contract arrangements

To some extent the above discussion depends on whether the landscape scheme is implemented as a sub-contract of the building contract or as a separate main contract. Yet even in the first case any possible cuts should always be referred to and agreed with the client. There is certainly a strong argument for hard landscape works being included in the building contract where most of the necessary trade skills lie. Dealing with all landscape works in this way has the advantage of one contractor being responsible for the whole project.

Where landscape works are a sub-contract however, top soiling is often undertaken by the building trades and can result, if unsupervised, in a 'clean' blanket of top soil over compacted or debris-ridden surfaces. There is much to be said for soiling being undertaken by those responsible for sowing, planting and establishing the soft landscape – in other words the specialist landscape contractor employed under a separate main contract. Shrub borders can be left 300 mm below finished ground level and grass areas 150 mm below. The builder's responsibility to leave a clean and tidy site, which must include the works area, is then self-evident and surface compaction can be remedied before soiling takes place. This arrangement allows for a much longer defects and maintenance period than would be acceptable in a building contract. It also affords greater potential for pupils' participation in the implementation of the landscape scheme.

It is a great advantage if the landscape contractor is fully responsible not merely for the growing medium but for early establishment over at least a 36-month period. Emphasis in the contract can then be more on performance and the achievement of an objective, rather than on completing a series of operations. Such long-term responsibility cannot but encourage higher standards at the outset. For this and other reasons it is equally important that the landscape architect's design aims and the school's use requirements are set down in a management plan. It should fully describe their objectives, both for the site as a whole and its individual parts. Such a plan could be devised from a checklist of criteria for considering the development and maintenance of outdoor education facilities at schools.

4.11 Existing school grounds

The process of enriching existing school grounds must recognise that teachers' time is limited, that they may need help in identifying the individual and unique qualities of their own site, that historically the grounds maintenance service may have been essentially negative and inflexible and that they may be concerned about the acquisition of resources to implement change. To be successful, especially over the longer term – and that is the objective – these various factors must be tackled. Specific issues and processes to consider before commencing the enrichment of existing school grounds are set out in the appendices. Figures 20, 21 and 22 provide examples of how advantage has been taken of existing site features.

FIGURE 20

**BRANTFIELD
NURSERY
SCHOOL, KENDAL**

**Adaptation of the
grounds around a
Victorian house**

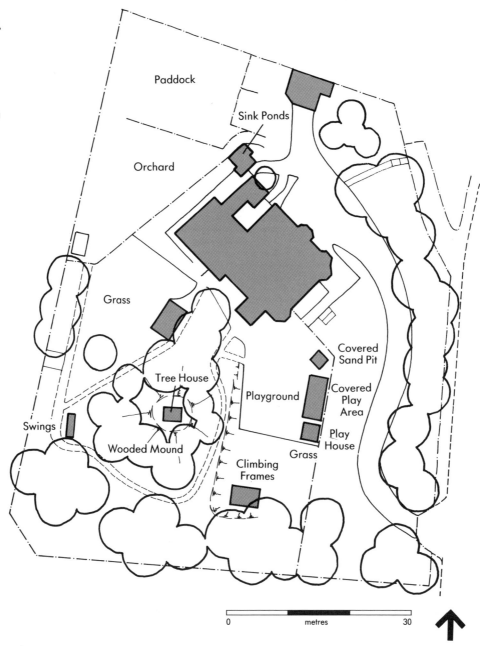

Paddock

Sink Ponds

Orchard

Grass

Tree House

Covered
Sand Pit

Covered
Play
Area

Playground

Play
House

Swings

Wooded Mound

Grass

Climbing
Frames

0   metres   30

Brantfield is not a purpose-built nursery; it is a three storey adaptation of a large Victorian family house on the outskirts of Kendal. The grounds have been changed by the Cumbria County grounds maintenance staff, and they now provide a useful resource for learning. The original owners had imaginative ideas about garden design and they had created interesting path systems incorporating a mound on the steeply sloping site, and these have been retained. The nursery is provided with a playground containing a covered sand pit to cope with a variety of weather conditions, water facilities for play, a separate covered play area adjoining a playhouse fitted with kitchen and dining furniture and fittings. On the top of the mound a treehouse is linked into the trees and to a platform/ lookout area. Elsewhere, there are timber climbing frames, swings and tableaux depicting Robin Hood and Treasure Island. Behind the house there is a tank pond, conservation area, and paddock on the hillside. An orchard has been planted which allows the children to harvest apples. The outdoor environment has been developed over a period of time and reflects the school's commitment to environmental education out-of-doors which extends and enriches the experience provided in the nursery.

50

FIGURE 21

**CRAWLEY RIDGE
MIDDLE SCHOOL,
CAMBERLEY**

**Adaptation of the
grounds of a
Victorian house**

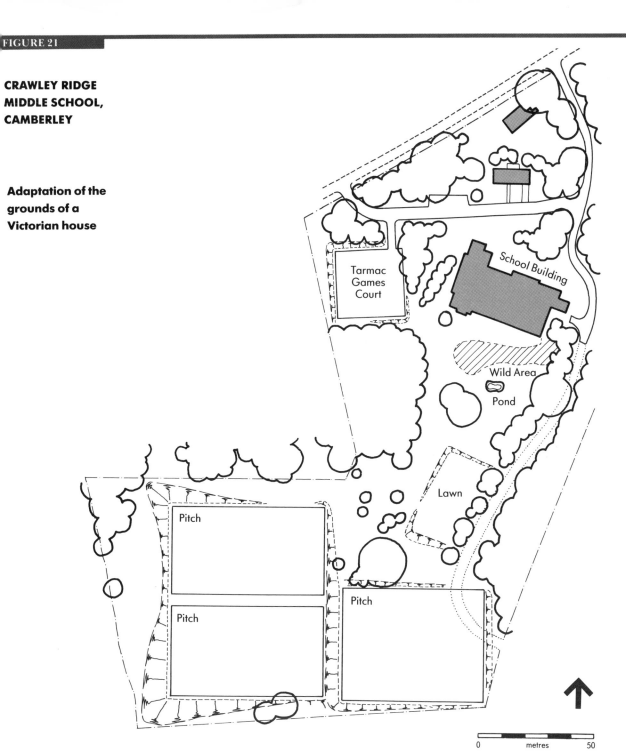

The school was built in the 1970s on the outskirts of Camberley. It enjoys the advantages of having been built in the well planted grounds of a former Victorian house. Every effort was made to preserve the trees and shrubs while creating hard paved games courts and grass playing fields. The building is multi-level to cope with the steeply sloping ground and the school makes extensive use of the original terrace which gives a commanding view of the gardens and playing fields below. The grounds have been so well endowed that there has been little to do except create a 'wilderness' area for wildlife and a pond with wetlands. The pupils have made miniplots and a project area to gain firsthand experience of growing plants and have built working models for experiements out-of-doors.

FIGURE 22

ST MARY'S HIGH SCHOOL, CHESHUNT

Preserving and developing existing features: A moat and site of an old house

School grounds often contain relics of the past, for example foundations of old buildings, old timber barns, ancient boundaries, disused railway track beds, and quarries. At St. Mary's High School, the grounds include a moat, the remains of a fortified house long since gone.

The school has turned the island site of the old house into a woodland nature reserve, and it has cleaned the moat and stocked it with coarse fish. It has kept alive a sense of history and given pupils the opportunity to be involved in a wide range of plant and wildlife studies.

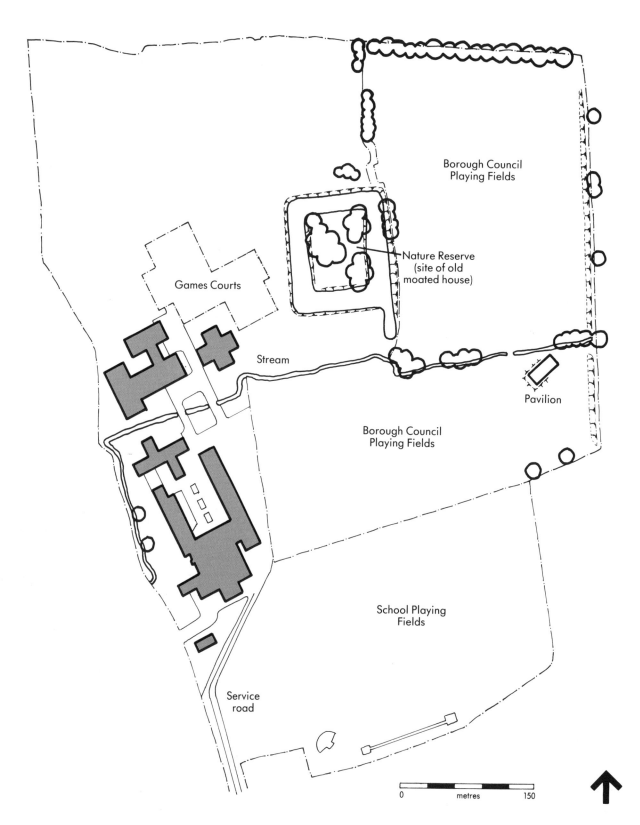

Borough Council Playing Fields

Nature Reserve (site of old moated house)

Games Courts

Stream

Pavilion

Borough Council Playing Fields

School Playing Fields

Service road

0   metres   150

FIGURE 23

**COOMBES
COUNTY INFANT
SCHOOL,
ARBORFIELD
CROSS**

**'Before
improvements'
(soon after
completion in
1971)**

See also Figure 24

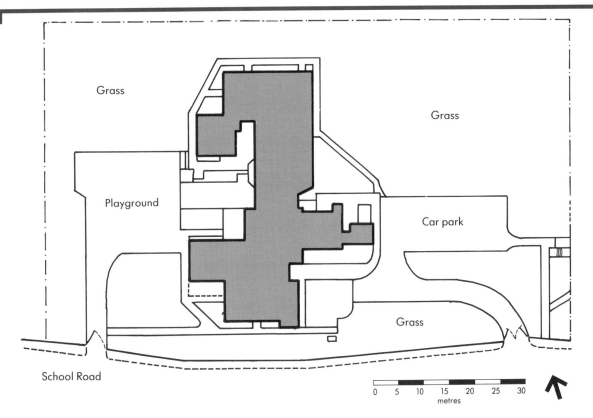

FIGURE 24

**COOMBES
COUNTY INFANT
SCHOOL,
ARBORFIELD
CROSS, IN 1990**

**'After
improvements'**
(change has been,
and remains, a
continuous and
evolving process)

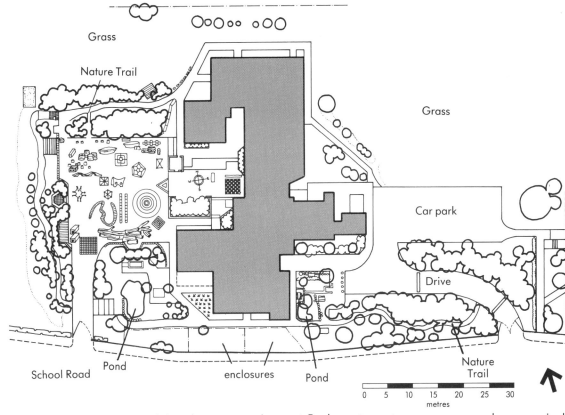

The school was built on the edge of the village in the early 1970s. When it was opened the grounds were a rather barren combination of short cut grass and tarmac. Over the last 20 years and at the rate of one outdoor project a term – tree and shrub planting in the autumn; pond, ditch or wall making in the other two terms, – the grounds have been transformed by teachers, the caretaker, pupils, parents and agencies into a teaching, learning and recreation environment. Funds for materials were raised by money-making school events, and through entering award schemes which provided cash prizes to create environmental curriculum-related grounds improvements. Enrichment of the grounds continues and features that are no longer required are reformed into new projects.

4.12 Contacts

Two of the most useful initial contacts are the educational and inspectorial service and the landscape architect or manager involved in promoting development of school grounds. There is every reason to establish early contact and find out who does what, but there is little value in rushing forward with vague requests for development of the grounds or an isolated resource. Invariably the reply will be 'Why do you need it?' or 'How does this fit into the overall site context and other potential demands?' or 'Have you discussed it with teacher colleagues and pupils?' These issues must be addressed in the school's preliminary planning.

4.13 Developing ideas

Thus, at the same time as establishing contacts and identifying their roles and relationships, it is valuable for the school to develop its own ideas about outdoor resources and their uses. Everyone should contribute – teachers, pupils, secretary, caretaker, supervisors, crossing attendants, parents, neighbours and wider community – and all suggestions, however extreme or obtuse, should be discussed and recorded. A site plan at a scale of 1:1250 or preferably 1:500 will aid this process immensely, as would a simple model. Schools can usually obtain plans directly from the Local Education Authority or the related Estates, Property or Architects' Department. Other essential information concerns underground services and details of the current landscape maintenance contract.

4.14 Site meetings

Before ideas become too specific it is preferable to meet either, and preferably both, the inspector/adviser and the landscape architect/manager. This will allow proposals to be developed in the unique context of the site. It will help if the school's ideas have been forwarded beforehand to those attending the site meeting. This could be a short written report, supported by a plan, which explains how the school has developed its ideas and what its objectives and priorities are.

It is important to survey and appraise all the existing and potential resources within and around the boundaries. They may already exist and have simply not been recognised. Alternatively, a small change may be all that is required, such as creating access to an existing wild area, to release a rich new teaching resource. Current site features might be adapted to more relevant and rewarding uses. Finally, new opportunities for teaching and learning could be created, based on the needs of the school and the potential of its grounds.

4.15 Plans and phasing

Options might include upgrading parts of the playing fields for better and more sustained sports use, thereby affording other areas for enrichment of educational opportunities across the curriculum, provided these alterations are consistent with the Education (School Premises) Regulations. It might involve digging up tarmac, importing topsoil, sowing seed and establishing plants. Trees and shrubs can divide the new areas, provide shade and shelter and form different sized spaces. It often means rationalising the pattern of access and circulation around the building. These various issues are best brought together in the form of a development plan that must be flexible, determining a range of possibilities and potential phasing of works. It should then avoid the inherent danger of pursuing one initiative which subsequently proves to have prevented a number of others taking place.

If successive years of pupils are to gain from the anticipation, planning and implementation of new initiatives, the grounds should be forever changing. One solution is to think in terms of, say, a five-year development plan, identifying what is proposed each year. It can be reviewed annually to match objectives with the availability of resources and ensure that all changes are picked up by the annual maintenance programme. In this regard the closest co-operation with the local grounds maintenance supervisor is essential.

Thorough recording, possibly in the form of a permanent diary for the site, will inform future teachers about what was done, why, when and by whom. The need for planning, consultations and the continuity of projects and management cannot be over-emphasised. A school ranger service would be an excellent way of complementing the teachers' input.

It may be that after two or three such development plans it is time to start afresh – to clear and replant ornamental shrubs to reshape areas, to coppice woodlands or lay hedgerows or even to rotovate and reseed wild flower meadows. All this activity offers far more scope for teaching and learning than just passive study of existing features. At the same time it is important to be opportunistic and not stick too rigidly to a preconceived plan or timetable if resources suddenly become available for a specific project.

4.16 Funding

Simple adjustment to maintenance regimes need not involve great additional cost and may result in small savings. Indeed the move towards a more diverse and less manicured landscape is unlikely to have significant revenue implications. The slight increase in costs resulting from smaller, more intricate areas can be offset by the lesser frequency, or absence, of operations elsewhere. The issue that every school must face is how to fund the capital cost of major change. If the proposals are directly related to the National Curriculum, the Local Education Authority may have a central fund under Local Management specifically for environmental initiatives. Guidance may also be available on grant aiding bodies, voluntary groups and possible sponsorship. A rolling programme of gradual improvement is an obvious use of limited resources, which might well afford greater educational benefits and more direct participation than sudden and complete change organised and implemented by 'outsiders'.

Community service, armed forces, employment or environmental initiatives, local and national voluntary or community groups may all be able to provide labour and possibly machinery, although in some cases there is a small charge. Secondary schools could help primary in the implementation of new projects. There are also the school's own resources, including its local management allocation and fund-raising activities, the latter involving Parent Teacher Associations who may themselves support environmental initiatives. The flexibility afforded by Local Management might underpin provision of more expensive facilities such as artificial sports surfaces via a partnership with the District Council or a local sports association. Such sharing of resources with the local community on a well planned and regulated basis rarely leads to conflict in time zoning of these various uses.

Whatever new initiative is contemplated by the school, the issue of subsequent care and management must be addressed and resolved before commencement. The most common cause of eventual failure has been the lack of provision for ongoing maintenance. It might not mean additional money, merely talking to and involving other people.

Management and Maintenance of the Grounds

5

5.1 Management and maintenance

Management plans set the broad objectives for development and use of the outdoor environment over the longer term. Maintenance involves day-to-day care of the grounds to achieve these ends. The prime mover must be the school, which should decide the pattern and intensity of activities and phased implementation of the related resources. There may be a need on heavily used sites for both space and time zoning. It is very important that positive action is taken to organise site usage and to monitor closely the condition of the grounds, otherwise there is a danger that maintenance procedures will determine educational use rather than the other way around.

Whatever is practised by way of landscape management will have environmental implications. For example, it may raise issues regarding the care of flora and related fauna which certainly demand discussion and a full understanding of the various options. The feasibility of a more organic approach, as against the convenience of herbicides, is an immediate and topical theme. The school must make these decisions but needs the advice and support of landscape staff to achieve and implement them.

5.2 Value of guidelines

Without specific guidelines and regular user involvement there has often been a clear tendency for grounds maintenance staff to pursue their own convenient and essentially unchanging maintenance regime. Work study and contract systems which lay greatest stress on the ways and times of doing things rather than the end result may well blunt initiative and discourage craftsmanship, besides supporting this static approach. There is a further danger that peripatetic landscape teams erode the sense of personal responsibility and commitment to the individual school, especially where they are swapped frequently from one area to another.

5.3 Specifying the work

Performance specifications, which set down what is to be achieved, have been encouraged by competitive tendering in preference to operations specifications, which define exactly when and how many times tasks are to be undertaken. They give more responsibility and flexibility to contractors by telling them what is wanted and leaving them to organise staff and machinery to these ends. In certain respects they are easier to supervise since standards for checking are always evident. If a performance specification is backed up by a user guide, rather than the actual contract documents, school staff can quickly understand what standards have been agreed, what to look for and whom to contact, and thus manage their own sites more effectively.

5.4 Grass areas

The maintenance of amenity grassland demands more input and presents more seasonal problems, especially at the peak of the growing season, than any other form of maintenance. There is also a great range of options with regard to the form and make of machinery. The choice of machinery directly affects output and consequent costs. Tractor mounted equipment is vastly cheaper than pedestrian mowers and this must influence, though not determine, design and management of grounds. There is a great temptation to deride the gangmower as the cause of green

FIGURE 25

MOLEHILL COPSE COUNTY PRIMARY SCHOOL, MAIDSTONE

Grounds maintenance regime changed to suite the curriculum

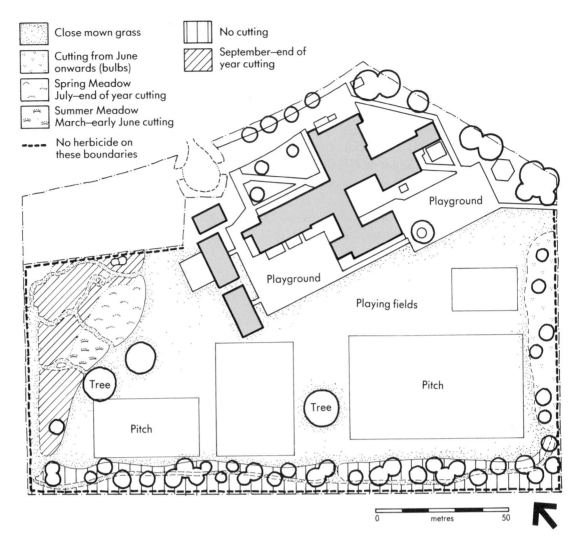

Key:
- Close mown grass
- Cutting from June onwards (bulbs)
- Spring Meadow July–end of year cutting
- Summer Meadow March–early June cutting
- No cutting
- September–end of year cutting
- No herbicide on these boundaries

Playground

Playground

Playing fields

Tree

Tree

Pitch

Pitch

Pitch

0   metres   50

Over a number of years, the teachers and pupils have planned new outdoor resources to match curriculum needs in partnership with grounds maintenance staff. They have reduced the amount of grass gang mowing which extended over the site by limiting the area of short grass to the games pitches. As a result of the reduction in grass cutting it has been possible to establish a nature trail, a copse with a variety of young trees, a pond, wetlands, and wild flower meadows. A new grass maintenance regime has been devised by the pupils to show the zones in the grounds requiring different kinds of grass treatment and the frequency of cutting to allow these resources to flourish and be an asset to the curriculum.

'deserts' in school grounds. Yet they can be extremely cost-effective for larger areas with good accessibility. They are, however, less suitable for sand carpet and sand profile pitches, and some damage may even occur to slit drained pitches. An alternative is a compact tractor fitted with a system of hydrostatic drive cylinder mower units.

Since the pedestrian cylinder mower is relatively expensive it is important that only those areas which demand such fine cutting on amenity or use grounds should be included. Difficult shapes, corners and steep slopes might be better planted up or mown less frequently. It is only when frequency of cut is reduced, which demands the use of a rotary or flail mower on longer grass, that savings can accrue. Extensive use of pedestrian machines may well be diminished by redesign or a reappraisal of the approach to annual maintenance. Reduction in mowing frequency, even if it does not make substantial savings because of the greater amount of time taken, will at least use less non-renewable resources and enhance habitat and landscape diversity. Even so, natural succession must be held in check to maintain such variety, and this requires some annual mowing to achieve management objectives.

Mowing some areas less often creates diversity in appearance and potential uses. Established wild flower meadows need one or two cuts per year and the cuttings must be removed to preclude enrichment of the soil. As a rule of thumb a single cut and collection equates with the annual cost of gang mowing. This is partly because collection on a horticultural rather than an agricultural scale has been very expensive. Better machinery or collection by the school would make the comparison more favourable. For convenient usage it is essential to mow pathways and larger gathering areas within the meadow regularly (Figure 25).

Another option is conversion of grass areas to woodland, and in this case the time-scale of actual savings depends on the relative costs of grass maintenance and tree planting respectively. Where grass mowing is expensive the costs of planting up a woodland can be recouped in as little as 5 to 10 years in the form of savings in the annual maintenance budget. Where it is exceedingly cheap, such as on large, gang mown areas, it may take over 40 years. It is thus in difficult corners, on steep banks and other areas which require pedestrian mowing that planting up with trees is likely to be most viable.

5.5 Shrub borders

Wider use of selective herbicides, and consequently less hand cultivation and failure to replace dead or dying shrubs or to cope with trampling and damage, have meant shrub borders are often a negative rather than a positive feature on the school site. There is every indication that many schools would prefer to see a smaller area of shrub border maintained to a higher standard. Given their current proliferation this might be a positive move in landscape terms, especially if it is balanced by more natural shrub planting amongst meadow or woodland. Such comments apply with more force to hybrid, floribunda or grandiflora rose beds, which demand an even higher level of maintenance but offer less in terms of educational use.

5.6 Hedges

These may be informal flowering shrubs, more formal ornamental varieties or the mixed native hedge, with establishment and maintenance costs generally decreasing from first to last mentioned. Informal hedges of flowering plants demand careful and more frequent pruning, whereas beech, hornbeam and more native hedges can be trimmed once a year. Native hedges are best kept in an 'A' shape for both ease of cutting and habitat value. Increasingly, tractor-mounted hedge trimmers are replacing hand-held mechanical trimmers, greatly reducing annual maintenance costs. A further option is to allow the hedge to grow on and lay it every ten years or so. This is another case where educational use and cost-effective maintenance may well be in harmony rather than in conflict. A phased programme of hedge laying on a large school site would allow pupils to be involved every year.

5.7 Trees

Tree management on the school site may extend from young plantations to mature specimens. In the former case a three-year, and preferably a five-year, maintenance programme is essential once planting has taken place, to ensure successful establishment. Herbicides can be precluded by use of a mulch, the easiest being a metre square polypropylene mat, provided it is securely anchored at the edges under the surrounding turf. Watering may well be necessary, especially in the first year. Stakes, ties, guards and any fencing will need regular, say monthly, inspections and occasional formative pruning may be beneficial. These tasks are all within the capability of the school, as indeed is most of the original planting, and it can afford great potential for teaching and learning.

When woodland planting is designed it is important to have in mind the management system – coppice, coppice-with-standards or high forest – and the prime purpose of educational opportunity. Coppice has the advantage of change and development, woodland products for school crafts and fewer demands on limited space or problems with the ultimate size of trees. The harvest cycle varies from one year for osiers, seven to ten years for hazel, 15 to 18 years for sweet chestnut and 30 years for hornbeam. Like laying a hedge, small areas could be cut each year. With mature trees on the school site the major issue is one of safety and at the very least there should be an annual inspection by a qualified arboriculturalist. Prevention is better than cure and each well-treed school site should have, as part of its landscape management plan, a phased programme of felling, replacement and, of course, additional planting. Absence of the latter encourages resistance to felling over-mature specimens.

5.8 Litter

This is primarily a case for good site management being enshrined in school policy. Whilst there has been inadequate provision of suitable closed-topped bins in the past, this does not solve the problem in itself. The main issue may well be a slackening of vigilance that can spread through the school to the point where the grounds reflect this prevailing, laissez-faire attitude. Once litter gathers it tends to proliferate. Mowing through litter strewn grass makes the problem much worse. It must be dealt with at source a school policy aimed at sustaining a sense of care and responsibility. Indeed, the source of the problem and the remedial measures may present a very useful project.

5.9 Competitive tendering

Under the Local Government Act 1988 local authorities whose expenditure on grounds maintenance exceeds £100,000 per annum must put it all out to competitive tender on a phased programme of 20% per year from 1 January 1990 until 1 January 1994. With a maximum length of four years, contracts will then be subject to regular re-tendering. Clear and totally separate 'client' and 'contractor' responsibilities have been established in local authorities. The former

prepare contract packages, specify work to be done and advise schools before and during the contract. The latter or private contractors undertake the work they have won, in accordance with the specification.

5.10 Size and supervision of contracts

The financial size of these contract packages has varied considerably. Larger contracts are easier to manage but may attract only a few often distant and non-specialist contractors. Smaller contracts involve greater problems of administration and supervision, but may provide a local, more specialist service. If the emphasis is on quality of service to the client, there can be decided advantages in smaller contracts, even to the point of arranging a contract for a single, but usually large, site. Schools may need to be more involved in day-to-day supervision and this development will further educational use of the grounds. Such involvement is a means of returning school grounds to their owners and users, but it does depend on sound technical advice being at hand.

5.11 A school ranger

The new 'client' groups should be seen in the same category as the advisory service, since their prime function is to provide outdoor educational resources. The landscape contract supervisor's remit needs to be far wider than merely checking contractor's work and should encompass liaising with and advising teachers and pupils on all aspects of grounds development and management. It demands working with the schools to implement change and directing the contract service to this end. The landscape contract supervisor thus becomes more of a school ranger, akin to the now familiar countryside ranger. The service requires user surveys to determine needs, regular liaison meetings with schools, news-sheets to promote ideas and maintain contact and the strengthening of links with the advisory service. They can work with teachers and pupils to plan new resources, to establish priorities, to support phased implementation and to advise on subsequent management plans on which annual maintenance can then be based.

5.12 Local Management of Schools

Many schools have more direct responsibility for the care and development of their site as a result of the Education Reform Act 1988. This provided for delegation of budgets to schools under a formula funding system and the freedom to shift expenditure across all budget headings. They have a tenant responsibility for the grounds and may spend more, less or just the same on maintenance of their site. Their main choices for implementation of this work are to join the Local Education Authority's grounds maintenance contracts, to employ their own private contractor, to establish a school-based organisation or possibly a combination of these options. Some authorities have already responded to Local Management by offering different qualities of service to schools via their centrally arranged maintenance contracts.

5.13 Options

A desire to spend less does not necessarily mean a reduction in educational opportunity. Indeed, the planting of trees and the establishment of meadows, with a reduction in close mown grass, shrub and rose borders, may well meet both objectives. Since the higher cost soft landscape elements are relatively small in area, the potential savings may not be as great as the differential maintenance rates suggest. Conversion to woodland or scrub, where appropriate and desirable, offers better opportunities for cost reduction in the longer term (Figures 26, 27 and 28).

Where a school wants to increase financial outlay on its grounds, it may also wish to become more fully involved and even take on direct responsibility. Thus it may decide to opt out of the authority's contract system, either partially or totally. Those tasks that demand expensive machinery, such as gang mowing, or specific skills, such as herbicide application, can continue to be bought in. Other landscape work can then be undertaken by groundstaff or a sports technician,

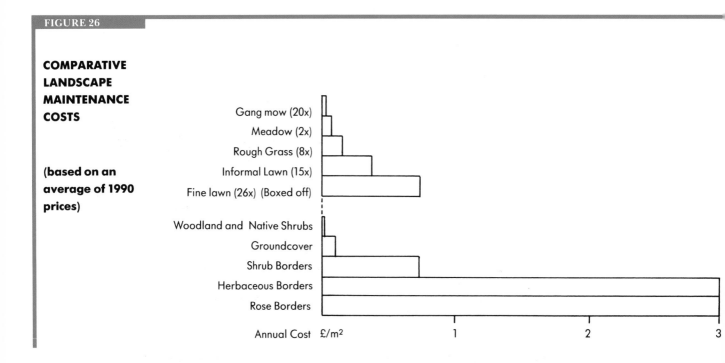

FIGURE 26

COMPARATIVE LANDSCAPE MAINTENANCE COSTS

(based on an average of 1990 prices)

Gang mow (20x)
Meadow (2x)
Rough Grass (8x)
Informal Lawn (15x)
Fine lawn (26x) (Boxed off)

Woodland and Native Shrubs
Groundcover
Shrub Borders
Herbaceous Borders
Rose Borders

Annual Cost £/m²   1   2   3

FIGURE 27

**DENMEAD FIRST
SCHOOL,
PORTSMOUTH –
CHANGING
DESIGN AND
MAINTENANCE**

(a) 'Before change'

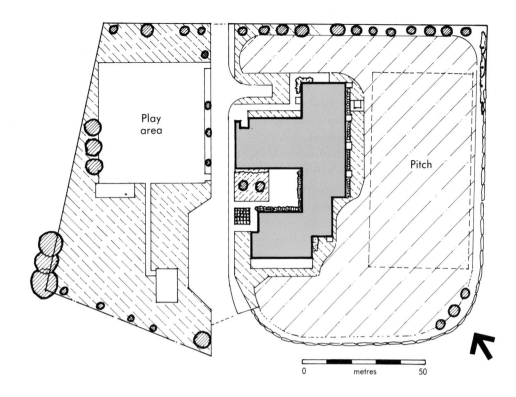

FIGURE 28

**DENMEAD FIRST
SCHOOL,
PORTSMOUTH –
CHANGING
DESIGN AND
MAINTENANCE**

(b) 'After change'

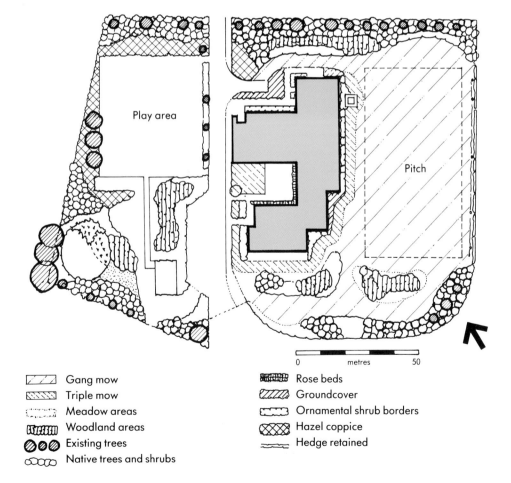

	Gang mow		Rose beds
	Triple mow		Groundcover
	Meadow areas		Ornamental shrub borders
	Woodland areas		Hazel coppice
	Existing trees		Hedge retained
	Native trees and shrubs		

Redesign of the grounds and changes to the maintenance regime can make savings in the annual revenue budget but this usually requires significant capital outlay on improvements.

provided that such an arrangement does not conflict with the requirements of the legislation.

5.14 An environment fund

Whilst schools can and will make gradual adjustments to the design and management of their grounds, substantial change is not provided for under formula funding. New landscape features and habitats, such as ponds or woodlands, provision of a range service, improvements to playing fields, greater provision for social and play areas, extensive storm damage costs and major repairs to fencing may not be fundable from the school budget alone. Such major expenditure could form part of the authority's mandatory element under Local Management, to be implemented via the advisory service working in partnership with landscape staff. Decisions could then be based on an assessment of individual school need within the context of the local authority and the demands of the National Curriculum.

5.15 A management policy

There remains the presumption outside the education service, and unfortunately sometimes within it, that the aim of grounds maintenance is essentially cosmetic. The provision of outdoor resources for education merits presentation in a management policy. It could be a statement of objectives by the LEA for all its educational establishments or by the individual school for its own grounds. An example is set out in Appendix 4.

By this means the multiplicity of educational uses in school grounds can be recognised and provided for. Failure to achieve such goals in the past has had much to do with a misunderstanding of objectives and a lack of knowledge amongst the various parties involved. Hence successful and sustained use across the curriculum depends very heavily on a close working partnership between all those concerned with educational use, design and care of the grounds.

Appendix 1
A Suggested Landscape Survey Checklist

The brief

Requirements of client, users and planning authority, with accompanying plans, reports

Land ownership/uses

Extent, lessees or tenants, covenants, adjacent owners, responsibility for boundaries, right to light

Easements/rights of way

Footpath, bridleway, road used as public path, access points

Wayleaves/underground services

Gas, water, electricity, telephone, oil, foul or surface water sewer

Relevant grants

MAFF, Forestry Commission, Countryside Commission, Local Authority

Planning requirements

Previous consents/refusals, relevant conditions, local and structure plan policies

Past developments

Record plans, reports, surveys and photographs

Statutory designations

Tree Preservation Orders (T.P.O.), Conservation Area, Site of Special Scientific Interest, Ancient Monument, Listed Buildings or features, other national or local landscape and nature conservation status.

Highways

Motorway, trunk or county road proposals, site roads' width, loading surface/construction, sight lines, turning/junction requirements

Geology/landform/soils

Solid/drift geology and soil maps, reports or surveys, trial hole information, agricultural land classification or detailed surveys

Climate

General weather information, details of local microclimate, air pollution

Water/drainage

Floodplain, liability to flood, field capacity, extent, nature of and limits on discharges, water pollution

Aerial photographs

Recent and past, vertical and oblique (for vegetation cover, evidence of ground disturbance/ancient monuments)

Historical records

Local library/museum, evidence of former uses/inhabitants and features/associations, archaeological or historical remains

SITE INVESTIGATIONS

Setting

Relationship to surrounding landscape, land uses and occupants (Note: wherever appropriate, detailed information below should extend beyond site)

Landform

Distinct changes of level, ridges/valley, high/low points, configuration and degree of slope

Water/drainage

Depth, visible quality, origin and speed of flow, streams, ditches, ponds, springs, wet flashes, badly drained or flat marshy land, outfalls, culverts, drainage falls

Microclimate

Aspect, sunny/sheltered areas, air drainage, frost pockets, damp hollows, severely shaded/exposed areas, wind funnels

Soils

Trial holes (machine dug), hand auguring or digging of pits, samples for analysis, depth of topsoil and subsoil, water table level

Vegetation

Size, species, form of growth, condition, location

Boundaries/surfaces/services

Fences, walls, gates, steps, ramps, retaining walls, roads, paths, paved areas, overhead cables, manhole covers

Access/circulation/rights of way
Location, type, alignment, intensity of use, potential for new/improved access

Transport/community facilities
Public transport, bus stops, railway stations, shops, toilets, local recreation facilities

Current use(s)
Agriculture, industry, commercial, housing, recreation, transport – detail of type, appearance, intensity

Environmental impacts
Current incidence/source, type/pattern of air, water and noise pollution

Visual appraisal
Views into/out of site (type/extent/quality), spatial division (contained and open areas), features and eyesores, zone of visual influence (where the site can be seen from), skylines and intermediate skylines.

DETAILED TREE SURVEY

Brief/aim of survey
Development site, T.P.O. record, safety/highway inspection, woodland management plan

Type/dimensions
Woodland, tree group, specimen, hedgerow; species, age, height, canopy spread (north, south, east and west); clear height, diameter at breast height (D.B.H.) and exact location of trunk

Visual appraisal
Form/shape (relate to species), visual significance (quality and character), implications of removal

Condition
Deadwood, dangerous limbs, fungal fruiting bodies, weak fork/abrupt bends, pruning wounds or basal cavities, soil cracks, damaged roots, pollards, perennial or target canker, crown foliage dieback

Legal/site issues
T.P.O. Conservation Area, planning condition, relationship to buildings/boundaries

Classification by condition code
Essential (green), desirable (blue), not essential (brown), not desirable (red).

Appendix 2
Possible Site Features

Sand-construction pitch
All-weather pitch
Orienteering trails
Archery area
Survival training area
Camping space
Fitness circuit/trim trail
Outdoor art areas
Amphitheatre/stage
Spaces for drama
Geological exhibits
Textured surfaces
Geomorphology demonstration area
Model landscapes
Hills and valleys
Different slopes and ramps
Contours marked on ground
Spot heights
Sundials
Compass
Large scale map
Weather station
Rock and soil profiles
Nature or theme trail
Technology project area
Waterwheel
Prehistoric hill-fort
Iron Age hut
2D and 3D shapes/patterns
Quiet areas for study/reflection

Husbandry

Vegetable plots
Flower beds/gardens
Plant containers/boxes
Trellis for climbers
Herb garden
Herbaceous border
Tree/wild flower nursery
Ornamental shrubs
Soft fruit
Orchards
Nutteries
Hop gardens
Annual cornfield
Greenhouse/cold frames
Smallholding
Animal enclosures/paddocks

Boundaries

Hedges
Hedgebanks
Walls
Fences
Ditches
Shelter-belts

Wetlands

Stream
Pond
Island
Bog/marsh
Waterfall/rapids
Stepping stones
Damp meadow
Wooden boardwalk

'Natural' habitats

Woodlands
Trees
Scrub
Shrubs
Spring/summer meadows
Moorland/heathland

Artificial habitats

Bird and bat boxes
Stone/brushwood/log piles
Corrugated iron sheets
Carpets
Compost heaps
Butterfly gardens
Dry stone walls

Play/social areas

Hard surfaces
Grass areas
Seat clusters
Sitting/social areas
Parents waiting area
Play equipment
Play markings
Ball wall
Boules/croquet
Sand pit
Play mound
Rubber tyres
Logs
Construction materials
Tables
Cooking/barbecue area
Huts/tree house
Covered play space
Arbours/mazes
Hiding places/den/refuge
Mobile play equipment
Movable furniture
Walls to sit on

Appendix 3
A Landscape Brief for a New School

1. THE OVERALL OBJECTIVE

For example: 'The creation of opportunities for teaching and learning, recreation, play, meditation and social interaction that span the whole curriculum, are available throughout the year and extend to all corners of the site and possibly beyond. A rich variety of spaces, colours, textures and patterns should provide exciting stimuli for imagination and enquiry. The layout should make possible rather than determine a wide range of uses, allowing both flexibility and potential for further development by teachers and pupils. The design solution should be cohesive and lively and make a positive and unique contribution to the local environment.'

2. CONSULTATIONS

There should be close liaison with new teaching staff both prior to and after occupation, so that educational use of, and demands on, the grounds can be fully explored. Fine tuning of the landscape scheme may well be required after initial implementation and both time and resources might be reserved for this. On new sites where teaching staff are not available for such discussions, the aim should be to achieve a flexible solution in the form of several distinct spaces of varying size, quality and character that can subsequently be developed or amended by the school.

3. SITE SURVEY AND APPRAISAL

Record all existing landscape features (especially landform, trees and other vegetation), make a thorough visual assessment (both within and outside the site), fully appraise the local microclimate and evaluate the opportunities and constraints they jointly present for site development.

4. OPTIONAL LAYOUTS

It is essential to sketch out potential options showing access, circulation and parking, buildings, hard play areas and pitches. The size, character and possible use of the outdoor spaces created by these options should be indicated and fully discussed with teaching staff prior to arriving at a preferred scheme.

5. SITE OF BUILDINGS

Building location should respect existing landscape features, respond to external views, promote energy conservation by awareness of microclimate and how it might be used to advantage or amended, provide easy access with a sense of arrival and direction and be used as a positive element in the creation of external spaces.

6. BUILDING CONFIGURATION, FABRIC AND SERVICES

Consideration might be given to the inclusion of an atrium, courtyard, recess, covered yard or veranda where they offer direct benefits for outdoor use. Allowance should be made for future expansion and the location of temporary classrooms. Exterior walls could be valuable for ball games or planting and their detailing in the form of colours, patterns and textures might present a further educational resource. Underground and overhead services should be co-ordinated to minimise impact on external design.

7. ACCESS AND CIRCULATION

Fluid linkage of internal and external spaces should be consistent with the overall pattern of educational use. Vehicles and pedestrians should be completely segregated with contrasting hard surfaces to define routes and full provision for disabled access throughout the site. There might be a distinct and visually contained area for service and maintenance vehicles, including a separate tractor access to the playing fields and sufficient routes for emergency vehicles.

8. CAR PARKS

The location and detailing of car parks should aim to reduce their impact on the site to an absolute minimum. In particular they should not dominate the main arrival and entrance points around the building, with a preferred location on the periphery being screened by existing or new landscape features.

9. SITE BOUNDARIES AND ENCLOSURE

Adjacent uses, educational needs, site management and subsequent maintenance should all be considered in determining the detailed boundary solution(s). Internal fences, hedges, trellises or pergolas might be employed to define spaces, separate uses and create features.

10. *HARD PLAY AREAS AND SURFACES

The different demands of formal games, active pursuits and less robust activities, such as imaginative play, relaxation, social interaction and discussion, should all be recognised in design and detailing. Equally there is a need for varied and stimulating colours, textures, patterns, shapes and sizes related to these demands. The intensity and direction of movements and congregation around entrances by groups of pupils should be catered for in terms of path width, alignment and edge detailing.

11. SITE FURNITURE

Ample seating might be included in a variety of spaces, from bays off the playground to small hidden niches. Imaginative and original designs might reflect the intensity of use and be in scale with the users. Wherever possible, incidental seating, such as low walls, might be considered. Tables/worktops, litter bins, lighting, signs and outdoor storage might be provided in strategic locations to facilitate educational use.

12. EARTH MODELLING AND SOILS

New landforms in scale and character with their surroundings might afford a range of slopes and features to further outdoor teaching, sport and play whilst fulfilling specific design objectives. Stripping, storage and placement of soils should be related to the varying demands of the different site uses.

13. *GRASS SPORTS AND RECREATION AREAS

These should accord with *Building Bulletin 28* including marginal areas, banks produced by creation of plateaux and the need for shelter or other landscape works. Pitch layout should take full account of the size, shape and potential use of residual areas and the proximity of public roads and footpaths which may require ballstop fencing.

14. *SOFT LANDSCAPE

Tree and shrub planting should aim to create a strong landscape structure which can define spaces, provide shelter and shade, filter dust, screen or direct views and afford specific features and habitats. Planting design should reflect the inherent character of the site and the objective of diverse educational use. There should be great awareness of the intensity and robustness of subsequent use and the general desire for low maintenance. Care should be exercised with the width, shape and edge details for shrub borders, so that they thrive amid such intense use.

15. **GROWING PLANTS**

There should be opportunities to raise and grow plants close to the school in tree nurseries, garden plots and orchard areas with a rich growing medium.

16. **KEEPING ANIMALS**

Potential should also exist for small enclosures and paddocks for pets and farm animals to be kept or to visit.

17. **ADVANCED WORKS**

Ideally, structure planting on sites in the building programme should take place as soon as the project is included and all works outside the building contract area should be implemented as soon as detailed proposals and budgets are approved.

18. **AFTERCARE**

The ease and cost of subsequent maintenance, with particular regard to earth modelling and planting, should influence but not constrain a landscape design aimed at maximising educational use. Capital works might include a minimum 12 month maintenance period for grass and 36 months for planting. A management plan should set down the design and use objectives and form the basis for the annual maintenance programme.

* With reference to the Education (School Premises) Regulations 1981.

Appendix 4
Management Policy:
Statement of Objectives

1. A diverse and stimulating environment that offers the broadest possible range of opportunities for educational use, with the flexibility to accommodate changing demands for outdoor resources.

2. A landscape setting of quality that is in harmony with, and makes a positive contribution to, its surroundings.

3. Outdoor teaching spaces that are both safe and secure, and conform to statutory requirements for sports provision and the physical environment, as set out in the Education (School Premises) Regulations 1981 and relevant planning legislation.

4. Spaces and facilities for all forms of play and social interaction during the school day, including both active and passive pursuits for groups and individuals.

5. An ability to accommodate extra-curricular social and fund-raising activities that are of benefit to the school and community wherever the need arises and the capacity exists.

6. The tailoring of annual grounds maintenance to the educational needs of the individual school.

7. A working partnership of inspectors, advisers, landscape staff and individual schools to achieve these ends and provide sustained support for change and development.

Within the framework thus created by the Local Education Authority, schools could develop their own policies for landscape management and the care and maintenance of the school site. They could then formulate plans to provide for the phased and long-term development of the school landscape. These should always be available to pupils and users of the grounds.

Bibliography

DES, HMI and Architects & Building Branch Publications

DES

The Education (School Premises) Regulations 1981 (SI 1981 No 909)
Animals and Plants in Schools: Legal Aspects (AM 1/89)

DES SAFETY SERIES

No 1 *Safety in Outdoor Pursuits*
No 4 *Safety in Physical Education*

HMI PUBLICATIONS

Primary Schools – Some Aspects of Good Practice

ARCHITECTS & BUILDING BRANCH
Building Bulletins

BB7
Fire and the Design of Educational Buildings (sixth edition)
BB28
Playing Fields and Hard Surface Areas (second edition)
BB67
Crime Prevention in Schools: Practical Guidance

Design Notes

DN11
Chaucer Infant and Nursery School, Ilkeston
DN13
School and Community (2)
DN17
Guidelines for Environmental Design and Fuel Conservation in Educational Buildings
DN18
Access for Disabled People to Education Buildings (second edition)
DN36
Secondary School Playing Fields: North-East Wiltshire

Broadsheets

BS9
School Sites: Recreation, Play and Outdoor Education
BS17
Playing Fields: Marginal Areas

Useful Organisations

Association of Community Technical Aid Centres Ltd
Royal Institution, Colquitt Street, Liverpool L1 4DE

Association of Playing Fields Officers and Landscape Managers
(current address available from the Sports Council)

British Association of Advisers and Lecturers in Physical Education
(The Secretary's address is given in *Education Year Book*)

British Beekeepers Association
National Beekeepers Centre, Stoneleigh, Kenilworth CV8 2LZ

British Trust for Conservation Volunteers
36 St Mary's Street, Wallington, Oxfordshire OX10 0EU

Central Council of Physical Recreation
Francis House, Francis Street, London SW1P 1DE

Council for Environmental Education
School of Education, University of Reading, London Road, Reading RG1 5AQ

Countryside Commission
John Dower House, Crescent Place, Cheltenham, Glos GL50 3RA

Environmental Education Advisers Association
c/o Education Department, County Hall, Truro, Cornwall TR1 3BA

Field Studies Council (FSC)
C J Baylis (Secretary and Treasurer), Central Services, Preston Montford, Montford Bridge,
Shrewsbury SY4 1HW

Groundwork Foundation
Bennett's Court, 6 Bennett's Hill, Birmingham B2 5ST

Institute of Groundsmanship
Wroughton Pavilion, Wroughton-in-the-Green Sports Ground, Milton Keynes, Buckinghamshire
MK6 3EA

Landscape Institute
12 Carlton House Terrace, London SW17 5AH

Institute of Leisure and Amenity Management
Lower Basildon, Reading RG8 9NE

Learning through Landscapes Trust
Third Floor, Technology House, Victoria Road, Winchester SO23 7DU

National Association for Urban Studies
c/o Canterbury Urban Studies Centre, The Canterbury Centre,
St Alphege Lane, Canterbury, Kent CT1 2EB

National Curriculum Council
15-17 New Street, York YO1 2RA

National Federation of City Farms
The Old Vicarage, 66 Fraser Street, Windmill Hill, Bedminster, Bristol BS3 4LY

National Playing Fields Association
25 Ovington Square, London SW3 1LQ

Nature Conservancy Council
Northminster House, Peterborough PE1 1UA

Natural Turfgrass Council
3 Fernands Parkway, Harden, Bingley, West Yorkshire BD16 1HZ

Royal Agricultural Society: Countryside Communication
NAC, Stoneleigh, Kenilworth CV8 2LZ

The Royal Society for Nature Conservation
The Green, Nettleham, Lincoln LN2 2NR

The Royal Town Planning Institute
26 Portland Place, London W1N 4BE

Sports Council (Play Unit)
The Sports Council, 16 Upper Woburn Place, London W1CH 0QP

Sports Turf Research Institute
Bingley, West Yorkshire BD16 1AU

Tree Council
35 Belgrave Square, London SW1X 8QN

World-Wide Fund for Nature UK
Panda House, Weyside Park, Godalming, Surrey GU7 1XR

Designed by COI and printed in the United Kingdom for HMSO
Dd 296463 C15 6/93 72958